'An unusual and fascinating book... Yvonne Ward has the percep-
tiveness to present in a new light what at first sight might seem a
well-trodden subject, deploying her own knowledge and archival
research to make a fascinating read by re-editing the editors.'

Literary Review

'Four stars – Yvonne Ward tells a complicated story clearly and
simply, which is the reverse of the normal academic procedure.'

Mail on Sunday

'Ward argues convincingly that Esher and Benson's radical pruning
of Queen Victoria's early correspondence has had a profound effect
on her posthumous reputation... a timeless reminder of how important it is for biographers to find the time, space and will to battle
back to the primary sources.'   *Guardian*

'Hats off to Yvonne Ward... who has exposed the gentlemanly networks that tried to hide the truth about Queen Victoria.'

Robert Lacey

'Yvonne Ward has done a sterling job of delving into history to
find out how the reputation which the Queen guarded so fiercely
during her lifetime continued to be manipulated and reshaped
even after her death – as well as how many myths continue to
persist even today.'

Lucinda Hawksley, author of *The Mystery of Princess Louise*

ABOUT THE AUTHOR

Yvonne Ward is a historian with a doctorate from La Trobe University. Her publications include the lead essay in a special edition of *The Court Historian*, published to mark the Golden Jubilee of Queen Elizabeth II. She lives in Victoria, Australia.

CENSORING QUEEN VICTORIA

HOW TWO GENTLEMEN EDITED A QUEEN AND CREATED AN ICON

Yvonne M. Ward

ONEWORLD

A Oneworld Book

This paperback edition published 2015

First published in North America and Great Britain by
Oneworld Publications, 2014
First published in Australia by Black Inc., an imprint of Schwartz Media Pty Ltd

ISBN 978-1-78074-654-8
eISBN 978-1-78074-428-5

Printed and bound in Great Britain by Clays Ltd, St Ives plc

Oneworld Publications
10 Bloomsbury Street
London WC1B 3SR
England

CONTENTS

PART II: THE QUEEN

To my family
and other teachers

Reginald Brett, 2nd Viscount Esher.

A.C. Benson

John Murray IV (seated) and his brother Hallam in their London offices, 1903.

PREFACE

QUEEN VICTORIA, AS SHE has come down to us, is the product of her biographers. For over sixty years these biographers did not have access to the Queen's original correspondence, which is held in the Royal Archives at Windsor Castle. They had to rely instead on the published selections of letters produced by 'royal command' of Victoria's son, King Edward VII, and her grandson, George V. The first of these selections appeared in 1907 and, in three volumes, covered the Queen's life until the death of Prince Albert in 1861.

I consulted this publication when I was writing about the Queen as a wife and a mother. The dearth of letters dealing with Victoria's personal and domestic life made me question the selection itself. Who were the editors and on what principles had they operated? The senior editor was Lord Esher, who was an influential figure in the court of Edward VII; his colleague was Arthur Benson, not so highly placed but very well connected. Both had known the Queen as a matron and matriarch – but what would these two gay men have made of the letters of a young woman, a young wife in love, a new mother? How much would they have understood of Victoria's dilemma as a female ruler: the challenges of being sovereign over men to whom she was meant to be inferior?

Such questions are not just a byway in the study of Queen Victoria. Esher and Benson's work still influences our view of the Queen. Their selections provided a template for the Queen's life and very few biographers have been able to escape their influence.

*

At her birth in 1819, Victoria was fifth in line to the throne. Her grandfather, King George III, had since 1810 been prevented from ruling by bouts of madness now attributed to hereditary porphyria. Her father was the King's fourth son, Edward; her mother was Princess Victoria, daughter of the German Duke of Saxe-Coburg.

The heir apparent was the King's eldest son, George, who served as regent during his father's illness. The line of succession continued down the family tree to the King's second son, Frederick, Duke of York, then to his third son, William, Duke of Clarence, then to Victoria's father, Edward, Duke of Kent. Next in line was Victoria, followed by the King's fifth, sixth and seventh sons. If George, the Prince Regent, were to remarry and produce an heir, that child would usurp all claimants in the line of succession, although this was deemed unlikely given his age, his health and his prodigious girth.

However, Victoria's position in the line of succession was to change rapidly. In 1820, when she was eight months old, her father suddenly caught cold, was treated by cupping and bleeding, and died. Within a fortnight, King George III also died, and the Prince Regent acceded as King George IV. The next in line, the Duke of York, developed dropsy and died of heart failure in 1827. On the death of George IV in 1830, the Duke of Clarence became King as William IV.

He had married Princess Adelaide of Saxe-Meiningen and they had several babies, but none had so far survived. If a child of his were to live, he or she would supplant Victoria's claim. Thus, during Victoria's childhood, becoming Queen was a possibility but never a certainty. It was not until the passing of the *Regency Act* in 1830 that she was formally deemed the heir apparent. Even then, the *Act* acknowledged the possibility that Queen Adelaide might yet give birth to William's child, even after the King's death. As the Secretary of the Privy Council, Charles Greville, explained, 'in the event of the King's death without children, the Queen [Victoria] is to be proclaimed, but the oath of allegiance taken with a saving of the rights of any posthumous child to King William'. That is, Victoria would be deposed from the throne should Adelaide subsequently give birth to a royal heir.

As it was, despite much speculation as to how to ascertain whether or not Queen Adelaide was 'with child', King William died without children in 1837. Victoria acceded to the throne one month after her eighteenth birthday. (The *Regency Act* also allowed for Victoria's mother, the Duchess of Kent, to rule on Victoria's behalf should she accede the throne before she was eighteen. Greedily, the Duchess and her comptroller, Sir John Conroy, had lobbied without success to have this extended until Victoria turned twenty-one.) When she became Queen, Victoria was barely 148 centimetres tall (or four feet ten inches) but hopeful that she might grow taller. Thanks to the training she had received as a child, whereby sprigs of holly were pinned to the neckline of her dress to improve her posture, she walked with a dignified grace.

In the third year of her reign she married her cousin, Prince Albert of Saxe-Coburg; they went on to have nine children before he died in 1861, aged forty-two. She died thirty-nine years and one month later, in January 1901, after reigning for more than sixty-three years.

*

These are the bare facts. Our impression of the woman behind them, however, has been distorted by the decisions of the men who compiled and edited the primary sources. By better understanding these men and their motivations, we can achieve a clearer view of the Queen and of how her story has been told.

PART I

THE EDITORS

Chapter 1

To Publish the Queen's Letters

On Victoria's death in 1901, Reginald Brett, the second Lord Esher, was charged with organising her funeral and the coronation of her eldest son, Edward VII. These tasks fell to him not because of the official position he held at court, which was minor; he was merely the Secretary of the Office of Works. But Esher had developed a reputation at court and in political circles: if a job had to be done well or if judicious advice was needed, Esher was your man. He was, as his biographer James Lees-Milne described, a person of wide and considerable influence, an advantage he maintained by refusing all offers of higher office. At various times he declined to be ambassador to Paris, the governor of the Cape (in South Africa) and the viceroy of India. He had been briefly an MP but refused to return to politics, even though he was twice offered a position in the Cabinet. He explained to his son:

It is not in my line to go back into politics and become identified with party strife. I can do more good outside, and heavens how much happier the life. Just imagine what the tie would be. I am purely selfish in the matter, and really I do not think I can bring myself to sacrifice all independence, all liberty of action, all my *intime* life for a position which adds nothing to that which I now occupy.

As the historian William Kuhn notes, his 'private life' had it been known would hardly have 'borne the inspection of his friends, let alone the public'. He was tempted by the offer of the governorship of the Cape, but eventually declined, recording in his journal, 'Were it not for Maurice I would go at once. As it is, I cannot.' Maurice was his son, with whom he was infatuated.

Esher inevitably became secretary of the Memorial Committee, which was charged with building monuments to the dead Queen and commemorating her life. With his understanding of theatre, Esher recognised the power of royal ritual and ceremony. Victoria had died at her summer residence, Osborne House, on the Isle of Wight. Esher canvassed the idea of the government purchasing the house from the King in order 'to keep it as a shrine, uncontaminated by domestic uses and to fill it with memorials to the Queen'. (Not only would this appeal to the masses, he suggested; it would also 'have a good practical effect on the King's financial position'.) Another idea was to construct a triumphal, ceremonial way to Buckingham Palace, with a monument to Victoria as its focus. This monument was finally unveiled by King George V in 1911; the project also entailed the construction of Admiralty Arch, a widening of the Mall and the redevelopment of the façade of Buckingham Palace, including the construction of the eastern balcony that has since become a stage for many royal events.

Esher was opposed, however, to the production of an official biography of the Queen:

Such a task is impossible during the lifetime of certain persons and until the shadow of passing events grows longer. Justice could not be done to the Queen's character, unless her later years were thrown into strong relief, for it was during her later years that her judgement mellowed, and her influence over her people and over the Empire became so powerful.

Esher had another idea, totally novel: to publish the Queen's correspondence. There have since been published volumes of the letters of various monarchs. But this was to be the first such collection, and it was to appear immediately after the demise of the royal letter-writer. Pondering the task, Esher recorded in his journal that 'the only possible thing to do was to (1) collect and arrange all her papers, (2) print selections from her journals up to a certain date, (3) print correspondence *very fully* up to a certain date'. The main purpose as he saw it at this stage was '*pour servir* the historians of the future'. This he believed would be 'far more interesting than any expurgated biography'. Indeed, 'the truest service to the Queen is to let her speak for herself'.

At this early stage he had some idea how prolific a correspondent the Queen had been. His plan was to publish her correspondence up to 1861, the year of Albert's death. To publish the correspondence 'very fully' even for this comparatively short period was to prove impossible, however. It has been estimated that Victoria wrote an average of two and a half thousand words each day of her adult life, and that she may have written sixty million words in the course of her reign. Giles St Aubyn calculates that 'if she had been a novelist, her complete works would have run into seven hundred volumes, published at the rate of one per month!'

Unique among British monarchs, Victoria had published edited extracts from her journals while she was on the throne. (In recognition of this, Disraeli, who himself was unusual in combining the positions of politician and novelist, flatteringly addressed her as 'We authors, m'am ...') *Leaves from the Journal of Our Life in the Highlands* (1868) was an instant success, selling twenty thousand copies and spawning several subsequent editions and a sequel in 1884. Letters between Victoria and the Dean of Windsor, Randall Davidson (later the Archbishop of Canterbury), show that the Queen had also wanted to publish a memorial to her highland servant, John Brown, following his death in 1883, but was persuaded to forego the project. In a masterfully subtle letter, Davidson outlined the likely public response to such a panegyric, noting that 'I should be deceiving Your Majesty were I not to admit that there are, especially among the humbler classes, some (perhaps it would be true to say many) who do not shew themselves worthy of these confidences ...' The Queen's children had never liked even the most innocuous confidences of the *Highland Journals* being made public, so were relieved when the Queen was persuaded by the Dean.

Victoria had appointed Princess Beatrice, her youngest child, as her literary executor, with instructions to destroy anything liable to 'affect any of the family painfully'. The Princess turned her attention first to her mother's journal, which spanned almost seventy years (commencing when Victoria was thirteen years old) and filled 122 volumes. Beatrice copied the entries into thick, blue-lined exercise books, censoring and altering as she went, and then burnt the originals.

She proceeded in this way for thirty years, filling 111 copybooks. These are held at the Royal Archives in the Round Tower of Windsor Castle and are now available online. King George V (Victoria's grandson) and Queen Mary tried to stop the destruction of the originals, but failed. The journal exists in its original form only until February 1840, although some later entries had appeared with the Queen's permission in the authorised five-volume biography of Prince Albert, published between 1875 and 1880.

Immediately after the Queen's death, Esher kept his plan to publish a selection of her letters secret. As a consummate political operator, he knew he would have to clear the ground, quite a lot of ground, to ensure there was no opposition from Princess Beatrice, Victoria's other children, the King or his senior courtiers. Esher needed to establish his credibility with each of them personally and within the court. He waited more than two years before he broached the subject with the King.

Within weeks of the Queen's death, however, he began to lay the foundations. Possibly after being given access to her papers in order to clarify matters of protocol for her funeral and the coronation, Esher observed that they 'were not well kept after the Prince Consort's death'. This was, he thought, due to the Queen's insistence on relying only on Prince Albert's German secretary, Maurice Müther, and on a cataloguing system, instituted by the Prince, that was incapable of dealing with the avalanche of papers over Victoria's long reign. At the end of April 1901 Esher recorded that he had, at last, had an opportunity to speak to the King about arranging the Queen's papers in a more orderly fashion.

The extent of Esher's access at this point is unclear, but he seems to have been rankling under restrictions. He expressed his frustration in his typically gentlemanly manner: 'The

King will possibly become less tenacious and secret as time goes on. It is impossible to avoid trusting a private secretary if a man, King or subject, wishes to be well served.'

The King was soon won over. During the months following Victoria's death, Esher quickly became a key figure in the domestic life of the royal family. In March he recorded that he had spent most days with King Edward and Queen Alexandra 'most intimately, fussing about their private affairs'. Much of the next two years were taken up with such arrangements. Between these duties and his role on the Memorial Committee, Esher was kept very busy – and in the process made himself the obvious man for the job of sorting the Queen's papers.

There was still, however, the problem of Princess Beatrice. It was not clear exactly how far Beatrice's responsibility extended – just to her mother's journals, or to all of her documents? That the King had asked Esher to arrange his mother's papers suggests that Beatrice's responsibilities rested primarily with the journals and perhaps also with 'private, family letters'. The King himself may have been uncertain. In October 1902, however, there was a breakthrough for Lord Esher. Princess Beatrice wrote to him, asking if he could spare some time to assist her: 'I feel I ought finally to go through all that remains for as I have my dear Mother's written instructions to be solely responsible for the arranging and retaining of them in the manner she would have wished, I must not leave it to others ...' Esher seized the opportunity to familiarise himself with the Queen's papers.

He soon realised that to produce a publishable collection for the reading public, he would need assistance. The ideal co-editor would be a scholar of literary attainments and would of course be a man, a gentleman, from a suitable social and educational background. The ideal candidate soon emerged.

Lord Esher had come to know Arthur Christopher Benson during his frequent visits to Eton College, where Benson was a housemaster and a close friend of Esher's own former housemaster, A.C. Ainger. Esher also knew Benson for the verses he had written for various royal occasions. 'Land of Hope and Glory' is the best remembered of these, originally written for the *Pomp and Circumstance March No. 1* by Sir Edward Elgar for the coronation of Edward VII. Benson was also a published writer, and it was his acclaimed biography of his father, a former Archbishop of Canterbury, that brought him to Esher's attention as a potential co-editor. After consultation with the King's secretary, Lord Knollys, Esher met with the current Archbishop, Randall Davidson, to discuss the project. Esher reported back to Knollys:

> [Davidson agreed] that *memoirs pour servir* in the shape of 'The Correspondence of Queen Victoria from 1837–1861' is what is required, connected more or less by notes and introductory passages, and that in reference to the editorship, Arthur Benson would be superior [to the other candidates] – more capable, more suitable and more trustworthy; [and] that it would be desirable, perhaps necessary, that I should be associated with him in the joint editing of the book.

The gentlemanly networks were in full swing. There were deep family and church connections between the Bensons and the Davidsons, and as Benson's biographer, David Newsome has described, Benson had become deeply discontented with his work at Eton. Davidson knew this and was able to tell Esher. But there were protocols to be observed. Esher had to ask Knollys for permission 'to privately ascertain if – <u>in the</u>

event of the suggestion being made – Arthur Benson would consent to undertake the task'. Knollys, in Dublin for the State visit of the King and Queen, replied that the King 'fully approves your sounding [out] Mr Arthur Benson as to whether, together with you he should be willing to undertake the work. Should he be so, you are at liberty to talk the matter over generally with him.'

Esher wasted no time in summoning Benson to his home, Orchard Lea, in Windsor. Benson had no inkling of the nature of the visit. He sent his acceptance but, like Eeyore, worried lest it should rain. In his diary he recorded the invitation from Lord Esher: 'the King wished him to speak to me on a matter of importance! It must be that Lord Churchill wants me to take his boy next year …' In accepting the invitation, he joked to Esher that he felt like a prisoner summoned to the guillotine: 'I am wondering what it can be that H.M. can want to have me spoken to about, as it feels as if I should be arrested by *lettres de cachet* and committed to the Tower!' In fact, he was to be taken captive by letters and committed to a tower – but to the Round Tower at Windsor rather than the Tower of London.

Benson 'byked' over to Orchard Lea and found his way in. Esher was in the garden reading with his son, Maurice, alongside him. Benson described the garden in full beauty and observed that 'in the whole of the long talk that followed, my thoughts and recollections are curiously knit with the colours and textures of flowers in the beds we paced past'. He had no premonition of what Esher was to ask him:

> Esher made me a statement at once, with a kind of smile, yet holding it back for effect. The King was going to bring out Correspondence and letters of Q.V. and would I edit it,

with him. (Esher). I was to be sounded and then offered it. He had seen the Archbishop who entirely approved.

This opportunity was something of a godsend to Benson, as he confided in his diary:

> Here am I crushed with work at Eton, hardly strong enough to wriggle out and yet no motive to go at any particular minute. Suddenly in the middle of all my discontent and irritability a door is silently and swiftly opened to me. In the middle of this quiet, sunny garden, full of sweet scents and roses, I am suddenly offered the task of writing or editing one of the most interesting books of the day, of the Century. I have waited long for some indication – and was there ever a clearer leading?

The afternoon continued with an examination of Esher's collection of biographies, another stroll, tea, listening to opera on a gramophone (a marvellous novelty to Benson) and further talk as Esher walked some of the way back to Eton with Benson. During this walk, Esher revealed more interesting snippets about the project, which Benson duly recorded in his diary. He was interested to learn that 'there are two rooms full of letters and papers at Windsor,' and that Princess Beatrice was 'engaged in copying from the Diary what she thinks of <u>public</u> interest' – which Benson supposed to mean 'the dullest part'. This rather bland description of Beatrice's task, omitting any mention of the original journals being burned, is intriguing. If Esher had told Benson about the burning, Benson would surely have said so in his diary. The omission suggests that Esher may not have known about Beatrice's incendiary activities at this stage.

Esher was pleased with his efforts and wrote the next day to Knollys, reporting that Benson was 'humbly grateful to the King' for his 'gracious proposal'. Esher also reported to Davidson that 'Benson seemed very captivated by the idea'. Davidson replied that he was sure Benson's appointment would be 'a wise one'. But Benson, despite his initial excitement, became unsure as darkness fell. Back at Eton, he sat through a meeting about fire precautions (there had been a fatality in a fire the previous month). The performance of the headmaster, Edmond Warre, disillusioned him further about the school's leadership, but he remained unsure what to do. He 'had a bad night – and no wonder – shirked Chapel, and then wrote two letters – one to Warre resigning as simply as I could – and one to Esher accepting'.

Benson's formal letter of acceptance was accompanied by a less formal one, which showed some of the traits that Esher's biographer, James Lees-Milne, says Esher found especially irritating. Benson began breathlessly:

> I don't see why I should keep you waiting any longer for the answer, which is <u>YES</u>. I had not really any doubt when you asked me, but one ought, like Robinson Crusoe, to make a careful list of the <u>cons</u> in a serious matter like this. There are one or two cons, but not to be weighed for a moment against the <u>pros</u> ...

And he continued:

> I enjoyed my visit to you yesterday very much and thought myself a great fool for not having been before; but I don't think that Fortunate Princes like yourself know the pangs of diffidence suffered by blonde persons of the Walrus

type! I want to say elaborately how grateful I am to <u>you</u>, whose kind hand I trace in this matter; but it is all there!

Yours ever,

Arthur C. Benson

Esher, according to Lees-Milne, 'looked on Benson as an over-credulous old woman' who fussed over details. Benson's letters were apt to be written as if he were flustered, in stark contrast to Esher's cool and polished tone. For Benson, minor items often preceded more important ones, which were frequently tacked on as afterthoughts, the opposite of Esher's to-the-point *modus operandi*. In the letter of acceptance quoted above, Benson added a postscript: 'One other minute point – may I mention in the circular I shall have to write to the parents the cause of my resignation?' One can almost hear Esher spluttering as he reached for his pen to provide some suitably oblique wording for the parents' circular. A royal appointment was not to be publicly announced in a note from a housemaster! Announcements of such importance had to be carefully planned. There must have been some further discussion on this point, as in a later letter Benson wrote:

I quite understand about not putting H.M.'s name forward; but it is a great relief to me to be able to speak freely about the work. To say I was leaving and then to nod and wink and jerk the thumb over my shoulder and say I would if I could &c. is not to my taste. Many thanks for making it all square.

Very sincerely yours,

Arthur C. Benson

Esher, with his experience of royalty and his awareness of the bigger theatre of Court, found Benson's myopia tedious.

Despite Esher's efforts, the news began to spread. On 1 August, Benson wrote again to Esher, telling him rather naively that he 'had told only two or three of my most intimate friends about the nature of the work I am undertaking, and they are sworn to secrecy, yet it is bound to get out – "a bird of the air will carry the matter" – and that would be a bore ...' Esher would not have wished to be held accountable for the news leaking before it was officially announced. On 15 August Benson reported that their mutual friend Edmund Gosse had told him 'it was a matter of common knowledge that you [Esher] had had the editing entrusted to you'. Meanwhile Esher's publisher, Frederick Macmillan, wrote to remind him that if a life of Queen Victoria was to be 'done', Esher had promised that Macmillans would be considered. Obviously a 'little bird' had flown and was now twittering freely along the branches of the gentlemanly networks.

Esher wrote to Lord Knollys, suggesting that a notice to 'dispose of unauthorized rumours' would be a good idea. He then wrote to his secretary, Stanley Quick, in London, with the wording for a formal announcement and instructions to 'Send a copy of the enclosed to *The Times* before 12 o'clock on <u>Saturday</u> morning and to all the principal papers, and to the Press Association so that it appears on <u>Monday</u>.' The message was succinct:

> H.M. the King has commanded the publication of selections from the correspondence of Queen Victoria between the years 1837–1861. The work will be edited by Arthur Christopher Benson M.A. and Viscount Esher K.C.B. and will be published by John Murray.

Two and a half years had passed since Esher had first conceived of the publication. Now that it was approved, he moved
quickly. At their first meeting, Esher had directed Benson to
organise a meeting with the publisher, John Murray. This
business, founded in 1768, was now in the hands of John Murray IV, who was reviving its fortunes. Another old Etonian –
he had been at school with Benson – Murray had published
several books about the royals as well as several of Benson's
previous works very successfully. When he and Benson met to
discuss Victoria's letters, just a week after Benson accepted
Esher's offer, Murray brought out ledgers to show how profit-
able his previous royal publications had been. The impres-
sionable Benson recorded: 'the *Speeches of the Prince Consort*
had been £1500 and the *Life of Princess Alice* over £5000. It
looks as if this ought not to be less.' They also discussed what
form the book should take. Murray recommended two volumes but allowed that three would be possible. There was no
mention of the projected number of pages or word length.
Murray recommended pricing the book at 42/-, or two guineas for two volumes. 'I liked sitting in his big, dingy panelled
room,' Benson told his diary with satisfaction, 'and being
treated with the respect due to a distinguished author.'

The contract between Murray and the editors (who were
referred to as 'the Authors') read:

> The entire proceeds of sales shall in the first instance be
> devoted to the repayment of the cost of the production; if
> after meeting this liability they yield a surplus all such
> surplus shall be treated as profit and divided between the
> Authors and the Publishers in the proportion of 2/3 to
> the authors and 1/3 to the publisher. If the cost be never
> covered by the yield, the publisher shall bear the loss.

On 21 August Benson accepted these terms and forwarded them to Esher. There was subsequently a separate agreement between the two editors. Esher proposed to Benson that:

> of our share of the profits you should take the whole up to £1200, and that of the nett profit over and above that amount you should take 2/3 leaving 1/3 at my disposal for any purpose to which I may apply it. Will you let me know if this suggestion meets with your approval, and if not what you would propose ...

These terms Benson accepted 'gratefully and unhesitatingly'. But he also understood that this was not mere generosity on Esher's part. In his diary he reminded himself: 'This means, of course, that I shall have to do all the work.'

Chapter 2

A PECULIAR GENIUS: THE SECOND VISCOUNT ESHER (1852—1930)

WHO WERE THE TWO editors? The first Lord Esher (1818–1898) was a newcomer to the aristocracy. He had made his name and fortune as a lawyer and married a French aristocrat. He became one of the Lord Justices of Appeal and was rewarded with the title 'Viscount Esher'. When his son, Reginald Brett, left for Eton, the first Lord told him: 'You will make your friends of nice, good, gentlemanly fellows and will not let anyone persuade you to do anything that is wrong … You will at every period of your life be thrown with the boys who are now at Eton with you …' Yet he cautioned: 'Remember what I told you that, as you and I were not born Dukes with large estates, we must work.' Regy did not learn to work hard at school, but he did make extremely useful contacts.

Esher's adolescence at Eton set the parameters of his life. His grandson, Lionel, wrote:

At Eton his charm, wit and good looks caught the eye of William Johnson (later William Cory). This remarkable teacher, who left under a cloud a few years later, implanted in his disciples the two complementary ideals of romantic homosexual love and high-minded service to the Empire. The model was classical Greece, the myth that of Achilles and Patroclus. Floating in a dodger on the silent Thames, then at the height of its elmy beauty, friendships were formed which were to last a political lifetime.

A modern reading would be that Johnson was a paedophile who groomed boys with his charm and used his rooms for procuration, sexual assault and voyeurism. But Esher and many of his contemporaries did not think of their boyhoods being spoilt; they wanted endlessly to return to their school-days. The eternal youth of Peter Pan epitomised this (Esher was a great fan of the play, which opened in London in 1904).

Regy went up to Trinity College, Cambridge, and took his degree in 1874, but he never recovered from having to leave the 'hedonist's paradise' of Eton. His grandson recalled: 'Years later, the recollection [of his departure from Eton] reduced him to tears.' His is a classic case of the syndrome Cyril Connolly described as 'arrested development – permanent adolescence' in public-school boys. Esher spent much of his time after Cambridge trying to recapture his boyhood, visiting and corresponding with William Johnson and other friends from those days. He even took a house near Eton with the writer Julian Sturgis, a popular and athletic old Etonian, where they befriended and courted new Eton boys, including the future Viceroy of India, George Curzon. While at Cambridge, Regy gave up a term in order to return to Eton and help Johnson following the latter's shameful departure (the parents of a student found a compromising letter from Johnson to their son, and Johnson was immediately dismissed).

After Esher left Cambridge, his father threatened to cut his allowance if he did not get a job. So at the age of twenty-two, he accepted without enthusiasm the position of private secretary to the Whig leader, Lord Hartington (the future Duke of Devonshire). Oscar Wilde's biographer, Neil McKenna, observed that there was something of a tradition of wealthy aristocrats inviting handsome young men to become their private secretaries, 'with all the ambiguities that surrounded such an invitation'. There were erotic possibilities in this relationship for men of homosexual or homosocial propensities. In the case of Esher and Lord Hartington, their letters suggest that by the time they parted, they had become more than employer and employee.

Esher's friends congratulated him on the appointment, welcoming it as a wise career move. Albert Grey wrote:

> As my father was Private Secretary [to Prince Albert and later to Queen Victoria] for a large part of his life, I know pretty well what this means ... the advantage of the position is this, that so long as you retain the confidence of your Chief, you will be the possessor of a whole host of interesting secrets, but beyond this, you will obtain an influence – the amount of which will be unsuspected from without ... It is the consciousness of this unacknowledged influence in which much that is of the highest importance, that makes the chief and dearest reward of a Private Secretary.

Another friend, Alfred Lyttelton, recognised that Esher had the diplomacy and discretion to make a success of the position:

You will now have a real opportunity of displaying what is your peculiar genius (for no other word expresses it) the great faculty you have for influencing people, upon a man who will be worth influencing, and this too in matters about which you have special knowledge.

Esher did indeed enjoy meeting influential people and speaking on behalf of his employer. According to the radical politician Charles Dilke, Esher conducted himself as though he 'held delegated authority from Hartington to represent Hartington's conscience when it would not otherwise have moved, and Hartington's opinion when the Chief had none'. Esher would later adopt a similar stance with Arthur Benson and John Murray, behaving as if he were representing the views of the King.

As a young man moving in the best circles in the 1880s, Regy was bound to meet the Prince of Wales, later King Edward VII. The Prince may have taken an interest in him because of their shared interest in horse racing, but the foundation of the Prince's confidence in Esher was the latter's role in averting a scandal involving the Prince's friend Lord Arthur Somerset.

Somerset was the second son of a Tory magnate, the Duke of Beaufort. He was also a member of the Prince's intimate circle, a major in the Royal Horse Guards, superintendent of the Prince's stables, an excellent horseman, an experienced soldier and an accomplished sportsman – seemingly the epitome of virile masculinity. In August 1889, he was questioned by police investigating a homosexual and under-age brothel in Cleveland Street, London. When the Prince of Wales heard the allegations, he was incredulous. 'I won't believe it, any more than I should if they had accused the Archbishop of Canterbury', was his first response. He later said that any man addicted to such vice must be regarded as an 'unfortunate lunatic'.

Anyone found to have visited a male brothel would face criminal charges. Somerset's friends were desperate that he not stand trial, where he might reveal not only details of his own visits to Cleveland Street but also the names of men who had accompanied him, or of the boys he had met there. The scandal would have brought the Prince's household and Somerset's regiment into disrepute. (The Prince's eldest son, the Duke of Clarence, was also implicated in the affair, according to the historian Theo Aronson.) Various cover-ups were effected, involving officials as high up as the Prime Minister. Somerset eventually escaped to the Continent, narrowly avoiding arrest.

Esher used his connections to keep the story out of the newspapers and to drum up financial help for Somerset, soliciting loans from men whose reputations were at stake. Over the next thirty years he collected his correspondence with friends and contacts about the affair, having it bound and stored in his extensive archive. He remained in touch with Somerset and with Somerset's parents for many years, which enabled him to reassure the royals that Somerset remained abroad. King Edward VII would have been well aware of Esher's ongoing role in avoiding a public scandal. The whole business was typical Esher. As the historian David Starkey has mused, Esher always 'emerged smelling of roses (but not too much)'.

Esher's own private life was intriguing. For anyone wishing to hide his homosexuality during this period, marriage was, as biographer Brenda Maddox puts it, 'the best closet'. In 1877 Esher's mother had urged him to marry, but he declared that taking a wife was 'one risk he would not like to take'. In 1878, however, his Eton mentor, William Johnson, married, and Esher had decided by early 1879 that he too should wed, writing of 'the icy shroud of matrimony which is creeping nearer and nearer ...' Perhaps he realised, as Christopher Isherwood later had a character explain, that 'being married does make a lot of things easier, because the world accepts marriage at its face value, without asking what goes on behind the scenes – whereas it is always a bit suspicious of bachelors!'

Young Regy had first met his future wife, Eleanor Van de Weyer, when she was barely thirteen years old. Nellie was the youngest of the four daughters of Sylvain Van de Weyer, the Belgian minister at the Court of St James. In her diary, with some perspicacity, Nellie discussed both Regy's character and her own ideas about marriage. She noted Esher's tendency to offer advice and help to people of influence and power; she wished that the same opportunities might be given to her too, but noted that 'men were not strong enough' to allow them. Two years later, in 1877 (while he was sharing a house with Julian Sturgis near Eton), Regy began visiting the Van de Weyers frequently; Regy and Nellie married in September 1879, when Nellie was seventeen. They had four children in quick succession: Oliver, born in March 1881, Maurice in April 1882, Dorothy in November 1883 and Sylvia in February 1885.

As a thirteen-year-old Nellie had declared, 'The greatest praise a husband of mine could give would be to say that he did not feel in the least tied down; or in any way encumbered than when he was a bachelor.' She was not to tie Regy down. Before their marriage, Esher hinted at his secrets:

Why you have thrown yourself away upon one who is the converse of you in all things still remains a mystery. Very sincerely I feel quite unworthy of you, and I think you must be a kind of St. Theresa, a reforming soul. Someday, like [George Eliot's] Romola, you will find me out and you will hate me. Are you prepared for this?

It astonishes me that I can write to you so easily and in this strain. You are the only girl with whom on writing I have felt on equal terms. I mean that I am sure of your not misunderstanding me and there is no necessity for elaborate detail. Does this please you or not? It is, I am sure, very unusual between a man and a woman who have anything to hide. True confidence is a very heavy burden and very few men and women can bear that of those they love. But you have led me to think you stronger than most women and I have very little fear for the future.

Do nothing and say nothing to weaken my faith in you … Do not, I ask you, start thinking too well of me, for I dread the disenchantment.

Throughout her life, Nellie carried this letter in her reticule everywhere she went. It may have been her credo, something which set out the rules as she had agreed to them and upon which she could rely, although she may well have only understood them by degrees as the years went on.

By alluding to secrets and double lives, Regy may have been preparing to exonerate himself from subsequent revelations. On the eve of their wedding, Nellie wrote to him, 'Do not think to frighten me with your two-sided character – show me which side you please. I should like you as much when your whole life was laid bare as I do now, when as you say, you humbugged me.'

Brenda Maddox has observed that women who accepted homosexuality in their husbands in this era tended to have particular traits:

> It is no accident that they choose homosexual men as husbands, unwittingly or not. As a type, they tend to be virgins when they marry or close to it. No critics of performance, but rather nice, plain girls, who want to have a home and children, who are sexually inexperienced and have never wanted sex so much that they could not do without it, and who are prepared to overlook a lot for a nice companionable man …

For whatever reasons, Nellie happily accepted marriage to Regy on his terms. She tolerated his dalliances, even welcoming into the household the various adolescent boys who infatuated him throughout their marriage.

Upon their wedding, Esher's employer, Lord Hartington, sent him a telegram expressing condolence rather than congratulations: 'When does your melancholy event come off?' From their honeymoon in Paris, Esher reassured Hartington: 'I am pretty well considering; not feeling much worse for the gloomy events of two days ago … I am beginning to feel that the worst is over … Marriage is a curious game to play at.'

Esher confided in his journal: 'It is difficult to describe the past ten days, sown as they have been with conflicting emotions', adding later, 'I have written *sub sigillo* [under seal] to my two best friends, an account of this first month of our married life.' During the honeymoon he also corresponded with one of his young paramours, Ernlé Johnson.

This would set the pattern for his epistolary activities and his relationships for all of his married life. If one obsession with an adolescent languished, he began another. Of longest duration was that with his youngest son, Maurice. It flourished when Maurice first went to Eton and continued for the rest of Esher's life.

Esher's obsession with Eton also continued, reaching fever pitch during the 1890s while Maurice was a pupil there. It seems Esher had a dual fixation with the boys and with the place. As many paedophiles before and since, Esher went to great lengths to contrive situations that would feed his fetish. Eton boys feature in almost every one of Esher's diary entries from this period and Esher haunted the college at every opportunity, seeking glimpses of his old favourites and scouting the new arrivals for potential paramours. He organised for a group of Eton boys to take part in Gladstone's funeral in 1898 and wrote in his diary, 'it was one of the pretty episodes of the ceremony'. For Queen Victoria's funeral, he persuaded the King to 'insist' that Eton boys had a 'privileged position', again extolling the beauty of the sight in his diary. In his rooms at Windsor Castle, which he and Maurice nicknamed the Nest, he filled a whole closet with Eton blazers. In 1902, when the King unexpectedly asked to be taken to these rooms to see some photographs of Maurice (who, at twenty, had just received a commission into the Coldstream Guards), he asked that the closet doors be opened and then wondered to whom all the blazers belonged. 'Fancy,' Esher wrote conspiratorially to Maurice, 'if you and the kids had been there, I should have conveniently lost the key.'

Esher bestowed on Maurice the pet name 'Mollie', which was also an old colloquial term for a homosexual man. While describing how he daily kissed the King's hand upon arrival and departure, Esher reassured Maurice that 'I only thought how little it all meant ... compared with a kiss upon another hand, and a few words of affection and appreciation from other lips.' When Maurice was twenty-five, Esher wrote to him:

> Dearest,
> I was very much hurt last night by your too obvious bore-
> dom, when I fetched you from the station. It was, I sup-
> pose, tactless of me, but as you must know, well meant.
> Whenever you are away, I look forward to your return,
> perhaps too eagerly, and I suppose I was a little too
> demonstrative last night …

Esher wrote many letters to Maurice of a romantic nature, recollecting intimate times they had shared as well as describing his activities at court; many of his views on the royals and politics have survived thanks to the deluge of notes he sent to 'Mollie'. As a schoolboy, Esher too had been assailed by letters from his father, who addressed him as 'My own darling Regy' and 'Darling of my soul' and demanded his company. Esher's father took him away on his court cir-cuits, travelling alone with him for extended periods of time until Regy was old enough to refuse. Contemporary research suggests that sexual abuse of children is frequently trans-mitted from generation to generation, and a boy who was a victim of homosexual incest may go on to become a perpe-trator. Esher may have been such a victim.

Esher believed that boys and men had needs and desires and were justified in seeking gratification; he saw no com-parable capacity or need in women and girls. Women existed to lavish affection upon him, and in return to be improved, charmed and educated by him. But he had accepted that there was a place for marriage in a man's life. In March 1907 he wrote to Maurice:

Dearest,

... By the winter you must have found someone to marry.
It will fit in well with your new existence ... it will give you
an anchor in life, and under conditions, which should
leave your great powers (for they are great) untrammelled.
You will throw yourself heart and soul into the details of
that great profession to which you belong, if you have safe
moorings at home, with a quiet harbour in which to lie,
untossed by distracting waves, and scattered before the
winds that blow round every one of us ...

In January 1911 Maurice finally married one of his
father's favourites, the beautiful, boyish actress Zena Dare
(she had impressed Esher playing Peter Pan in Manchester).
They eloped to a registry office in London, which Esher
found 'rather romantic'. He continued to write nostalgic
poems to Maurice, yearning to go:

Back to the sunny days that never more may be,
Just a little longer let me wreathe your hair,
Just a little longer let me hold your hand ...

'No human relations were ever much more perfect than
ours,' he reminded his son.

His eldest son, Oliver, and his two daughters, Dorothy
(an artist who eventually lived with Frieda and D.H. Lawrence in New Mexico) and Sylvia (who married Charles
Vyner Brooke, the last Rajah of Sarawak in Borneo),
enjoyed little attention from Esher, whose preference for
Maurice had long been obvious to all of them. Oliver did
not discover the truth about his father's relationship with
Maurice until after Esher's death, whereupon he wrote a

short but bitter book but decided not to publish it, according to his son, Lionel.

Esher's friendships, love affairs and fixations were always to dominate his life, but he accepted an ever-increasing number of offices and trusteeships of the second order – none of which took him away from London or Maurice. He was Secretary to the Office of Works from 1895 until 1902; from 1901 he was Lieutenant-Governor of Windsor Castle; he was appointed to the South African War Inquiry Commission in 1902; he became a director of the Royal Opera House from 1903 and was the King's nominee on various bodies including the British Museum, the Wallace Collection, the Commission of the Exhibition of 1851 and later the London Museum; he was the Chairman of the Committee on War Office Reconstruction from 1904; he was made a permanent member of the Commission of Imperial Defence from 1905; and he was the Keeper of the King's Archives from 1901, although the position was not made official until 1910. All of these positions were royal appointments; not one was elected. In December 1901 he was offered a partnership in Cassel's financial house at a salary of £5000 a year and 10 per cent of any profits. Although he resigned from Cassel's after two years, finding the work not to his taste, he remained on friendly terms with the Cassel brothers, one of whom was an intimate friend of the King.

In 1896, writing as Reginald Brett, he had published a book, Yoke of Empire: Sketches of the Queen's Prime Ministers. In handling the emotionally charged subject of Prince Albert, as well as Victoria's relationships with Benjamin Disraeli and William Gladstone, Esher solidified his reputation for discernment and discretion. Gladstone wrote to congratulate him:

Dear Mr Brett,

I have now read your book with real interest and pleasure. To dispose at once of the part in which I am personally concerned let me say that, were I to raise it absolutely in my own cause, I should issue from the ordeal with less to the Credit and more to the Debit side than you have liberally awarded me.

I cannot but regard as the central object of interest in the work the relations between the Queen and Lord Melbourne in the early years of her reign. But elsewhere, I think, as well as there, you have exhibited much care, tact and good taste.

Gladstone also wrote to the future King, recommending that he read Brett's book, but, according to Sir Sidney Lee, there were 'few signs that his anticipation was fulfilled'.

Esher was not without his critics. The German Emperor, objecting to an assessment Esher once made about naval shipbuilding, referred sarcastically to Esher's experience at the Office of Works, querying 'whether the supervision of the foundations and drains of the Royal Palaces is apt to qualify somebody for the judgment of Naval affairs in general'. Benson quoted a contemporary in his diary, meanwhile, who lamented:

'What is there he doesn't do? He has a great financial position in the city; he spends all his days smoking with the King; he reorganises the army in his intervals of leisure and now he is editing this vast mass of documents ...'

By the time Esher began editing Victoria's letters, however, he was well established as a Court favourite. He met

33

frequently with the King and Queen. He lived most of the time at Orchard Lea and had his own rooms within Windsor Castle. He also kept a house in Mayfair and had built a retreat, 'Roman Camp', in the Scottish Highlands near Balmoral. He maintained a huge correspondence and a complex social life with friends from both sides of politics, from Eton and Cambridge, through his various London club memberships and his associations with the military establishment.

When Esher died in 1930, his will stipulated that his papers not be opened for fifty years. His grandson Lionel remembered: 'His library darkly panelled and lined with his portentously secret correspondence was out of bounds at all times.' Here, among many other items, was the specially bound volume of papers on the Cleveland Street brothel, which could have destroyed many men, including several royals. Maurice was appointed his literary executor and edited the first two volumes of Esher's journals and letters, which were published in 1934. Upon Maurice's death the same year, his older brother, Oliver, decided to complete the work, and so discovered the real nature of their relationship. Selflessly, Oliver still prepared the third and fourth volumes for publication in 1936. Esher's deepest secrets, however, remained hidden until 1986, when James Lees-Milne published his biography, *The Enigmatic Edwardian*.

Esher's complex private and public lives are revealing: they tell us much about his perception of men, women and children, his ideas about domestic life, and his obsessions with pleasure, influence, beauty, knowledge and information. Although he declared that the Queen's published letters should project Victoria's own voice, his penchant for secrecy, and the intricate gentlemanly networks through which he maintained his position of power, prevented this. They influenced all of Esher's decisions, from the selection of Benson as co-editor to his assessment of which materials were fit for publication. Such extreme secrecy and unrelenting control are not the qualities an historian would wish for in the editor of a key primary source. Yet it was through this filter that the Queen was to 'speak for herself'.

Chapter 3

IT'S VERY REMARKABLE:
A.C. BENSON
(1862—1925)

ARTHUR BENSON WAS ALWAYS introduced as the son of his father. Edward White Benson had made a dazzling rise from schoolmaster-priest to Archbishop of Canterbury, despite having been orphaned at sixteen, the son of a bankrupt chemical manufacturer. He had a short career teaching at Rugby with Dr Arnold before being selected as the first headmaster of Wellington College, a new school being created under royal charter. He worked closely with the Prince Consort to establish the new school, and Queen Victoria maintained a keen interest in the college after Albert's death.

Edward married his cousin Mary Sidgwick. They were a well-connected family: Mary's three brothers all went on to become Oxbridge dons, and one married the sister of a future Prime Minister. As Edward's career progressed, both Mary and Edward developed networks of influential friends and colleagues. Thus Arthur grew up within the most eminent circles of Victorian and Edwardian England. He later recorded a conversation with Sir Philip Burne-Jones, the son of the artist Edward Burne-Jones, about 'the difficulty of being sons of famous men, and how it overshadowed one with inevitable comparisons'.

Born in 1862, Arthur was the second son of Edward and Mary's six children. After attending Eton and then King's College in Cambridge, he returned to Eton as a housemaster for twenty years. He became a fellow and, later, the Master of Magdalene College, Cambridge. He was a published writer of poetry, biography and memoir, and a member of the Athenaeum Club and of the Royal Society of Literature and the Academy of Letters. He was a friend of the Master of the Queen's Music, Sir Walter Parratt, and wrote verses and hymns for Queen Victoria and other royals. In 1904, when he began work on Victoria's letters, he was unmarried and forty-two years of age. Despite his many achievements, Benson sadly described himself as 'a good case of an essentially second-rate person who has had every opportunity to be first rate, except the power to do so'.

Benson's own personality and achievements were inextricably linked with those of his family, especially his father. In his biography of Arthur, David Newsome described the father, Edward, as having a 'prodigious physical energy and intellect, [with a] self-righteous and domineering personality'; he was a 'constant and imposing presence' in the lives of his children. In his diary Arthur wrote, 'Papa was, of course, strict, severe and moody, and believed in anger as the best way of influencing people – and he never knew how terrible his anger was.' He expected his children (and his wife) to be perfect; they must be examples of their father's principles in action and models to the boys in his care. They must spend all of their time in useful and improving occupation. Arthur recalled the books he was given to read: no novels, as writing fiction equated to telling lies, but 'books like *Philosophy in Sport*, where the boy cannot even throw a stone without having the principles of the parabola explained to him with odious diagrams'. The children never knew which innocent remark or act of childish impetuosity might be taken seriously amiss. The eldest son, Martin, came close to achieving perfection in his father's eyes but died when he was seventeen. As the biographer Brian Masters puts it, the remaining children were 'constantly reminding themselves what a disappointment they must be to their revered, faultless, fierce and dominating father'.

Arthur's mother, Mary (or 'Minnie'), was the only surviving daughter of the Reverend William Sidgwick, a second cousin to Edward. Reverend Sidgwick had been the headmaster of the Skipton Grammar School in Yorkshire but died of consumption in 1841, just two months after Mary's birth. In a state of prolonged bereavement, her mother eventually settled her family in Rugby, so that her sons could attend school there. Edward Benson joined the Sidgwick household in 1853 upon his appointment as a master at Rugby, and in 1859 he and Mary were married. The same year, he was appointed headmaster of Wellington College, which had just been built on a desolate heath near the criminal lunatic asylum of Broadmoor. This is where Arthur Benson spent his childhood.

Arthur was always much more at his ease with his mother. He was born in the third year of their marriage, when Mary was twenty and his father thirty-two. In contrast to Edward, Mary was tender, light-hearted and sympathetic. Arthur's letters to his mother during his years at Eton are much more expressive than anything he could have written to his father. They show him relating to her more as a peer than as a mother. For example, as a twelve-year-old, he wrote:

39

> WRETCHED MOTHER
> > GRACELESS REPROBATE
> > This is from your pining son whose bones are starting
> through his skin, who can neither eat nor drink for want of
> > YOUR LETTERS.
> > If the writing is not legible, it is probably owing to the
> tears which are steeping the paper at this instant.
> > Yet though so wasted by not getting your letters, I have
> managed to
> > PASS

Arthur later recalled that as children, 'our relations [with our mother] were perfect. We trusted her, we turned to her for everything; she was the gayest and liveliest, as well as the most perceptive of companions'.

The children were also very close to one another, perhaps because of their father's ferocity. None of them married. In adulthood, the two sisters gravitated to female networks, and all three of the Benson brothers were most comfortable in predominantly male surroundings. To assume the role of paterfamilias as discharged by their father was inconceivable to them. They could see no connection between romantic love and the emotional and material demands of women. In their youth they all experienced passionate friendships with their contemporaries and with older males; as adults they maintained many of these friendships, but constantly looked for companionship with increasingly younger men. By the age of thirty-five, Arthur had already discounted himself from being able to continue the Benson line and thought it lost unless his novelist brother, Fred, could be persuaded to marry. Only homosocial circles could provide the Bensons with the type of company they craved. The youngest brother, Hugh, sought it in the Roman Catholic church; Fred in literature and leisure; and Arthur in public schools, universities and literature.

Arthur's literary output was prodigious, running to over sixty published volumes. He was occasionally made the butt of satire by his family, which he took in good part. In 1906 his sister Maggie wrote to their brother Hugh:

> Did you see 'Signs of the Times' in *Punch*?
> 'Self-denial week. Mr A.C. Benson refrains from pub-
> lishing a book'!

In addition to his published books and family memoirs, Arthur maintained a diary for almost thirty years. It comprised 180 volumes, calculated by David Newsome to be more than four million words. Seven years after commencing the diary, he confessed:

> I reflect that, intimate in some ways as this diary is, there
> are at least two thoughts often with me, that really affect
> my life, to which I never allude here. I suppose people's
> ideas of privacy differ very much ... I don't think my sense
> of privacy is very general – but it is very strong about one
> or two things – and I have a carefully locked and guarded
> strong room. Anyone might think they could get a good
> picture of my life from these pages but it is not so.

Benson demonstrated the same capacity to keep things hidden in his published works. Brian Masters has observed that Benson often concealed emotionally laden episodes behind writing that was 'bland, truthful but completely locked against the inquisitive'. His treatment of the courtship and marriage of his parents, which he described in his biography of his father, was typical.

Edward Benson, at the age of twenty-three, had fallen 'hopelessly and devotedly in love' with Minnie, who was then just eleven; she was 'a fine and beautiful bud,' Edward wrote rather pruriently in his diary. Then, according to Fred Benson's transcription of the journal, Edward took 'refuge in cipher' before continuing his account:

> It is not strange that I should have thought first of the possibility that some day dear little Minnie might become my wife. Whether such an idea ever struck the guileless little thing herself I cannot tell. I should think it most unlikely.

The following year, Edward went to live in the Sidgwick household of his widowed cousin. He was studying at Rugby to take orders and was only required to teach one hour each day. He 'desired Minnie's company constantly, was never happy away from her and dreamed of nothing else but of some day making her his wife'. He tutored her and wanted her to accompany him on his frequent horse-rides and walks, which created tension within the household – she was still a little girl. Edward waited another year before he asked Minnie's mother if he could speak to her on 'The Subject'. In his diary, he described the proposal in lengthy detail:

> Let me try to recall each circumstance: the arm-chair in which I sat, how she sat as usual on my knee, a little fair girl with her earnest look, and then [I] got quietly to the

thing, and asked if she thought it would ever come to pass that we should be married. Instantly without a word, a rush of tears fell down her cheeks, and I really for a moment was afraid. I told her that it was often in my thoughts, and that I believed that I should never love any-one so much as I should love her if she grew up as it seemed likely ... [Accepting Edward's handkerchief] she made no attempt to promise, and said nothing silly or childish, but affected me very much by quietly laying the ends of my handkerchief together and tying them in a knot, and quietly putting them into my hand.

Ambitious young men grooming 'young girls to adorn the blessed position of their future wives' was not unusual, but only rarely were the girls this young. Once they were married, Edward continued to take Minnie on his lap, par-ticularly when he was finding fault with her. Yet he also sought emotional refuge in her company, casting her as a more mature, wifely figure, like Coventry Patmore's 'Angel in the House'. In his black depressions, he longed to 'lay my head on your breast and be comforted', surely a bewildering role for a young girl-wife.

Soon after their marriage, Edward and Mary were living in a new house in the grounds of a new school where Edward, an inexperienced headmaster, was trying to bring the staff and boys up to the exacting standards of the Prince Con-sort. At home, Mary was dealing with servants, budgets, sex, pregnancies and babies.

Arthur read his father's diary in preparation for writing his biography but declared the entries 'too sacred for quota-tion'. In the two-volume book he took just one paragraph to describe his parents' courtship and marriage:

And here I must touch, however gently, upon what was the central fact of my father's life – the companionship of my mother. From the time when he was at the University, and played with her as a little child, he desired some day to make her his wife. When he came to live with the Sidgwick household at Rugby, and, in the intervals of his school-work, found time to teach her, this desire was formulated not only to himself but also to others. Before he began his first independent work, when she was just eighteen, they were married, and the camaraderie of the Rugby house-hold was exchanged for the close companionship of mar-ried life among the wild and heathery solitudes of Wellington. Thus her life was bound up with his in a way which is seldom possible to a wife. There was not a single thought or plan or feeling which he did not share with her: and from first to last her whole life and energies were devoted to him. For many years she was his sole secretary. He consulted her about everything, depended on her judgement in a most unusual way, and wrote little for pub-lic utterance that he did not submit to her criticism. My father had an intense need of loving and being loved; his moods of depression, of dark discouragement, required a buoyant vitality in his immediate circle. One cannot con-stantly recur to the fundamental facts of life, but without a knowledge of this it would be impossible to understand my father's character and career.

Arthur's limited and rather adolescent understanding of adult heterosexual relationships is shown in his simplistic belief that there 'was not a single thought or plan or feeling which he did not share with her: and from first to last her

44

whole life and energies were devoted to him'. Arthur glossed over and perhaps did not comprehend the suffocating effect of the childhood courtship and the inherent loneliness, for Mary, of 'the close companionship of married life among the wild and heathery solitudes of Wellington'. What was he then to make, as editor, of the young Victoria's passion for Albert, or her need for companionship and love? Of 'bad nerves' after the birth of her second baby, or even of Albert's sense of isolation?

While writing his father's biography, Arthur had no knowledge that his mother had written a diary. It contained her anguished recollection of the courtship and the emotional pain within the marriage. She described her sense of entrapment, having been married at such an early age. She believed this had stifled the growth of her feelings for Edward and her ability to express such emotions. She longed to satisfy her masterful and demanding husband but her lack of heterosexual feelings, and anxiety about having left her mother alone, tore at her. Her account of their honeymoon in France and Switzerland, written in a fractured style many years later, poignantly expresses her attempts to make sense of the events:

> Wedding night – Folkstone [sic]– crossing – Oh how my heart sank – I daren't let it – no wonder – an utter child … danced and sang into matrimony, with a loving but exacting, a believing and therefore expecting spirit. 12 years older, much stronger, much more passionate! And whom I didn't really love – I wonder I didn't go more wrong …
>
> Paris – the first hard word about the washing – But let me think how hard it was for Ed. He restrained his passionate nature for 7 years and then got *me*! this unloving

childish, weak, unstable child! Ah God, pity him! Misery –
knowing that I felt nothing of what I knew people ought
to feel. Knowing how disappointed he was – trying to be
rapturous – not succeeding – feeling so inexpressibly
lonely and young, but *how* hard for him! Full of all reli-
gious and emotional thoughts and yearnings – they had
never woke in me. I have learnt about love through friendship. How I cried at Paris! Poor lonely child, having lived
in the present only, living in the present still. The nights! I
can't think how I lived.

Although Mary began the diary seventeen years after her
wedding night, the emotion was still palpable. One of the
few complete sentences was: 'I have learnt about love through
friendship.' The one thing Mary was certain of was her emotional debt to other women. Indeed, the diary was begun as
a cathartic self-examination on the advice of a new friend,
Mrs Mylne. Mary went on to establish passionate relationships with several women of high spirituality. After Edward's
death in 1896 she set up house with Lucy Tait, daughter of
the previous Archbishop of Canterbury.

Arthur and his brother Fred read their mother's diaries
together in August 1923, as they sorted her papers following
her death. 'She was afraid of Papa (I don't wonder),' wrote
Arthur, 'and it must have been terrible to be so near him
and his constant displeasure … In fact this little record
changes my whole view of their relations … probably they
should never have married.' He did not ponder what effect
his parents' relationship had had on him. He knew himself
well enough: 'My own real failing is that I have never been
in vital touch with anyone – never either fought with anyone
or kissed anyone! … not out of principle, but out of a timid

and rather fastidious solitariness.' He did not know or care to explore the cause.

During the ten years after 1892, Arthur published on average one book a year and during the following decade this rate more than doubled. These included gentle little prose collections, containing gentle reflections on nature and philosophical themes, which sold well, particularly amongst female readers. But he also wrote about individual men's lives, their characters and achievements. The men he chose were exceptional, mostly unmarried, or men for whom marriage was 'a closet' in Brenda Maddox's sense. He became something of a champion of homosexual and ambivalent men. In 1923, the year before his death, Arthur recorded a conversation with his brother Fred:

> We discussed the homo sexual [sic] question. It does seem to me out of joint that marriage should be a sort of virtuous duty, honourable, beautiful and praiseworthy – but that all irregular sexual expression should be bestial and unmentionable. The concurrence of the soul should be the test surely?

The novelty of the term 'homosexual' is evident in Arthur's writing of it as two separate words. He believed that men should be judged according to their depth of feeling, not social conventions or legalities. This was especially apparent in his biographical writings and in his celebration of the lives of men, many of whom he knew to be of 'irregular sexual expression'.

These books were published with neither fanfare nor secrecy, but sympathisers would have identified the encoded messages. Benson's first book, published under the pseudonym Christopher Carr, was *Memoirs of Arthur Hamilton, B.A. of Trinity College, Cambridge, extracted from his letters and diaries, with reminiscences of his conversation by his friend Christopher Carr of the same College*. It was published after Benson's return to Eton as master and he was soon identified as the author. The memoir described a love affair between two Eton boys. Such friendships, Benson wrote,

> are truly chivalrous and absolutely pure, are above all other loves, noble, refining, true; passion at white heat without taint, confidence of so intimate a kind as cannot even exist between husband and wife, trust as cannot be shadowed, are its characteristics.

But the affair painfully disintegrated when the boys were reunited at Cambridge, thwarted by guilt and a crisis of faith.

Benson's second book was a collection of biographical sketches called *Men of Might: Studies of Great Characters*, written in collaboration with his lifelong friend and fellow Eton master, Herbert Tatham. Published in 1892, this volume was written as a teaching aid, aiming to supply schoolmasters with 'lectures on men of various eras and denominations for boys 15 to 18 years old'. The subjects chosen were 'Socrates, Mahomet, St Bernard, Savonarola, Michael Angelo, Carlo Borromeo, Fenelon, John Wesley, George Washington, Henry Martyn, Dr Arnold, David Livingstone, General Gordon, and Father Damien, the leper priest of Molokai'. Benson and Tatham's mission was to instil in boys (and any other readers) a sense of glory in manhood, of the faith men could have in each other, and of the love and moral strength they could give to one another. Their collaboration itself grew out of a quintessentially homosocial friendship that began in boyhood and lasted for thirty-five years, until Tatham's death in a fall in the Alps in 1909.

Benson was writing at a time when there was a culture of homosocial and homosexual literature and publishing. Examples included the *Yellow Book*, the Uranian poetry movement and the journals of individual men. In 1897, both Benson and Esher were among the twenty-three subscribers to the publication of the *Journals of William Cory*. We met Cory previously as William Johnson, the Eton master (and Esher's mentor) dismissed in 1872 for indecent behaviour with a student. The *Journals* collected Cory's accounts of his romances with men and boys. Later, in 1902, Esher sent Benson four large volumes of Cory's letters to read. Benson wrote in his diary:

> They are deeply, wonderfully, moving and fascinating. The extraordinary mixture of shrewdness, knowledge, & dryness with abundant passion and sentiment. The high estimation in which he held the intellect – and yet ... The letters about the boyfriendships are very touching. It is odd to be surrounded, as we still are, by all this charm and not to feel it. But those lost and haunting *purences* of whom he writes – those boys with serene eyes ... with low voices full of the fall of evening ... they stand in these pages in a magic light of which no mortal would ever have for me ... I almost wish it were not so; if one could passionately idealise, like Newman, how much happiness ... how much pain ... and no one sees the dangers more clearly than I do.

Benson himself had published poetry expounding the beauty of boys and of boys' friendships, almost always in a lyrical tone of sad recollection. In 'A Song of Sweet Things That Have an End', he wrote:

Heart speaketh to heart
    Friend is glad with friend;
The golden hours depart,
    Sweet things have an end.

When Benson was asked to write an introduction to a collection of Cory's poems, he agreed. The result bordered on hagiography, further demonstrating his ability to be 'bland, truthful but completely locked against the inquisitive'. He celebrated Cory's influence and downplayed the behaviour of his dismissal:

> There are many men alive who trace the fruit and flower of their intellectual life to his generous and free-handed sowing. But in spite of the fact that the work of a teacher of boys was intensely congenial to him, that he loved generous boyhood and tender souls, and awakening minds with all his heart, he was not wholly in the right place as an instructor of youth ... He began to feel his strength unequal to the demands made upon it; and he made the sudden resolution to retire from his Eton work.

Benson knew the reasons for Cory's departure and obliquely hinted at them:

> ... with William Cory the qualities of both heart and head were over-developed. There resulted a want of balance, of moral force; he was impetuous where he should have been calm, impulsive where he should have been discreet.

Despite his own liberal views, Benson did not offer any anachronistic defence of Cory's relationships with boys. But by linking his name with Cory's poems, he did much to popularise them. This poetry provided inspiration to *aficionados* who themselves became Uranian poets, many of whom had been Eton boys themselves.

In his biography of the art critic Walter Pater, Benson considered the impact of classics education on the sexuality of young men:

> ... if we give boys Greek books to read and hold up the Greek spirit and the Greek life as a model, it is very difficult to slice out one portion, which was a perfectly normal part of Greek life, and to say that it is abominable etc etc. A strongly sensuous nature – such as Pater or [John Addington] Symonds – with a strong instinct for beauty, and brought up at an English public school, will almost certainly go wrong, in thought if not in act.

Tim Card, the historian of Eton College, wrote that Arthur Benson was 'like all the members of his gifted family, a depressive and a homosexual ... yet during his time at Eton he kept pederasty and depression at bay'. This was not without difficulty. In his diary Benson recounted that while doing his nightly rounds to speak to each of the boys, he stood unnoticed, watching as a maid tucked one of the students in. 'The boy was prattling away with intense amusement and interest ... I envied the boy's maid,' he wrote. Benson poignantly described this sensation as 'heart-hunger'.

He knew himself to be longing for love but incapable of intimacy. His writing was a means of bridging this abyss. Through biography he could bring a life into the public domain and engage with his deceased subjects in a pseudo-closeness, without the emotional risks of real life. Reading the Queen's letters created a very particular sort of intimacy for him: a trespass-by-invitation; a private view of a life that was already publicly known; but necessarily a one-sided experience, and one hampered by his limited experience of women.

Four days before Victoria's death in January 1901, Arthur Benson had joined a huge crowd outside the Mansion House to read the bulletins of her illness. Taking recourse to the language of chivalry, he wrote in his diary:

> It is curious how personally affecting it is. The thought of my dear liege lying waiting for death is a background for all my thoughts – and it gives me the same sort of anxiety that I feel for a near and dear relation.

It is not surprising that Benson should allude to the feudal relationship of lord and servant, or that he should have felt the Queen's decline so acutely. He had written words for hymns at her request; he had dined with her; his family had received condolences from her; and she had shown great kindness to his mother. Following Edward Benson's death in 1896, Victoria had invited Mary to Windsor, offering her consolation and even accommodation. In 1899, on the occasion of the Queen's birthday, some Eton boys had sung to her from a courtyard at Windsor Castle outside her breakfast room. Their program included a verse specially written by Benson and he was afterwards presented to the Queen, an experience he found surprisingly moving:

> I appeared bowing and drew as near as I dared.
> 'I must thank you for having written such a beautiful verse,' she said. 'It has been a great pleasure to me!'

I bowed and withdrew rather clumsily, as I had forgotten the backward walk and only remembered it after a moment – however I did not quite turn my back on the Queen I think … But what was an <u>entire</u> surprise to me & will remain with me as long as I live was her voice. It was so slow and sweet – some extraordinary <u>simplicity</u> about it – much higher than I imagined it & with nothing cracked or imperious or (as imitations misled me into thinking) wobbly. It was like the voice of a very young tranquil woman. The phrases sounded a little like a learnt lesson – but the <u>tone</u> was so beautiful – a peculiar genuineness about it; I felt as if I really <u>had</u> given pleasure … Tho' if I had had the <u>choice</u> I would not have dared to go, I am now thankful to have seen her and had speech from her. And is it absurd to say that I would cut off my hand to please her.

Although this deep emotional connection remained with him as editor of Victoria's letters, Benson was not enamoured with royalty *per se*. He could be scathingly critical of the people and practices of the Court, especially of King Edward VII. On attending a play at Windsor Castle, he commented:

The Windsor Uniforms are silly looking things. And the pussy cat manners of the men in-waiting [some of whom had been his Eton and Cambridge friends] all rather feeble … The royals came at length. The King with the 'irresistible bonhomie' look which I so particularly dislike. The Q. of Italy very disappointing – a coarsening Albanian! The King like a little dwarf. Our Queen very beautiful but a little haggard. My Duchess marched in, looking plumper and more matronly than ever; a crowd of nonentities, like Lorne [husband of Queen Victoria's daughter, Louise]. (What a figure!)

Benson was thus not mindlessly in thrall to the royals. Nevertheless, a royal commission was a powerful thing.

Benson regularly had vivid dreams, which he carefully recorded in his diary. None was more remarkable than the one he described in August 1923, soon after accepting another royal commission, this time from King George V and Queen Mary:

I was to have lunch with the King and the Queen, but on coming into a large saloon where I was to meet them, they had gone into lunch. A huge hall with many people. The Q. waved her hand to me, and the K. beckoned me to a small side-table where he had turned down a chair. He said, 'You see I have kept you a place. The Q. wanted to send up to you, but I said we wouldn't disturb your writing.' Then after a little he said, 'Do you ever reflect that I am the only king who ever inherited all the virtues and none of the faults of his ancestors. I have the robustness of the Normans, the activity of the Plantagenets, the romance of the Stewarts and the common sense of the Guelphs.' Then he said, 'I want you to look at the roof of my mouth. That will show you. That is how you tell a well-bred spaniel.' He turned to me, threw his head back and opened his mouth – but I could see nothing except that it was of enormous extent, cavernous and dark. I said I couldn't see, and he called an attendant who brought on electric torch. Then I saw it was as black as jet. I thanked him and he said, 'I particularly wish you to look at the roof of the Queen's mouth – do so afterwards.' I said I could hardly do that, but he said, 'Tell her I wished you to do so.' Events followed which I can't recollect, but I was eventually in a small sitting-room with the Queen, who said, 'Mind, it is only because the King desires it that I show you my mouth.' She threw back her head, and it was an enormous cavity of a dark purple, as if enamelled. I said, 'It's very remarkable,' and she said with a smile, 'You are right. You are about the only person to whom we have ever shown our mouths!' This did not appear strange or ludicrous – only a solemn privilege.

Dreams can have many interpretations. A literal interpretation of this one might be that the King was George V and the Queen was Mary, and the narrative a fantastic conflation of the many meetings Benson had recently had with them. It could also be, however, that the King represents Edward VII ordering Benson to 'look inside' Queen Victoria – which he did, metaphorically, by selecting Benson to read her letters. That Benson should dream of King Edward having an 'unfathomable' mouth and Victoria one that was royal purple yet 'enamelled' – and thus impermeable and unrevealing – might convey something of what he felt as editor.

The dream might also reflect Arthur's paradoxical view of himself: he was socially eligible to be invited to dine with the King and Queen but was offered a side table, alone; he was recognised as a writer but was not important enough to be left undisturbed; he was intimate with monarchs, yet even with assistance he could perceive very little and produced no significant insights from the experience, merely a platitudinous remark.

Just prior to this dream, Benson had been commissioned by George V and Mary to write *The Book of the Queen's Doll's House*, explaining and promoting the elaborate creation (designed by the architect Edwin Lutyens and completed in 1924, this miniature house was furnished in immaculately realistic fashion by leading British craftsmen, complete with flushing toilets and electric lights). Arthur thought the whole scheme 'ineradicably silly', but it was his first royal commission for a long time and he did not refuse it. He recognised that in frequenting royal circles, he had been given rare opportunities. Similarly, in editing Queen Victoria's letters, he was given a unique chance to gain an intimate view of royal life. He was anxious that he should produce something special, a work that would be hailed with more enthusiasm than that bland climax of his dream: 'It's very remarkable.'

Chapter 4

PREPARING THE GROUND

BOTH BENSON AND ESHER came to the project as published authors, but their ideas about how their work should proceed differed significantly.

Esher was familiar with some of the published and unpublished correspondence of the Queen from researching his books *Footprints of Statesmen* (1892) and *The Yoke of Empire* (1896). Meanwhile Benson's experience as a biographer, and his conversations with other writers at the Athenaeum Club and at Cambridge, made him aware of the many challenges involved in archival work. When the eminent historian George Prothero told him that there were many letters from Victoria to Lord Panmure (a minister in the government of Lord Melbourne) in private hands, it occurred to him that the letters in the Royal Library at Windsor Castle might only be a small portion of the Queen's words. Although there was a tradition that letters from the monarch should be returned upon the death of the recipient, many were retained as family treasures. Benson may even have remembered some held by his own family. He knew there must be many more throughout Britain, Europe and the Empire.

With this in mind, Benson suggested tentatively to Esher that perhaps some efforts should be made to locate and inspect such letters. Benson wanted to present as much of the Queen's character and personality as possible, more so than Esher. Esher apparently rejected the suggestion, which provoked a spirited defence from Benson.

Eton

Sept 17, 1903

My dear Esher,

Many thanks for your letter. Of course it would be absolutely impossible for direct application to be made, as from the King, to the holders of the letters, thus risking a refusal. But I should have thought that a notice in the papers couched in general terms would have avoided that contingency, and at the same time given the possessors of interesting and valuable letters the chance of putting them at the disposal of the Editors. The notice I mean might run as from you or even myself and say that the Editors would be much obliged if anyone possessing letters or papers bearing directly upon the period would communicate with &c …

It would be a great pity if people who were <u>willing</u> to lend interesting documents – and there must be many in existence – were not invited to do so. I do not myself see any strong objection to this course. It commits no one to anything, it is in no way undignified and it risks nothing while at the same time it gives possessors of valuable documents a chance of putting them at our disposal.

It also safeguards those who are responsible from the criticism of incompleteness which may be made if no opportunity is given to people, who would have been quite willing to do so, to send in such documents. But I say all this merely from the point of view of a biographer, who is anxious to let all possible material [be admitted] – and I would add that the national and historical importance of the book justifies even <u>more</u> care than usual in this respect.

But I need hardly say that I shall entirely acquiesce in the wisdom of whatever the King decided.

Ever yours,

Arthur Benson

Benson's diary entry concerning this incident moved from a tone of confession, to rage, then self-consolation:

I have made a small *faux pas* by suggesting that we should insert a notice to ask for letters. Of course it is the only thing to do if you want to get a good biography – but he [the King] won't hear of it, says Esher … the idiotic pomposity of monarchs! I must not forget that Esher though very pleasant & a real friend to me, will not hesitate to sacrifice me & throw me over at any moment. He cannot play except for his own hand; & I may be quite sure that if there are any disagreeable responsibilities to take or any harsh things to say, I shall be represented as saying them – I don't think I mind.

On the same day, he wrote again to Esher: 'I quite understand. My suggestion was made simply from the point of view of a professional biographer, anxious to lay hands on all available material. But I quite realise that there are other considerations of counterbalancing importance.' Despite such humiliations, Benson kept testing the boundaries, usually without success.

Benson expected the work to commence promptly, but Esher appeared to be in no hurry. The new school year had started at Eton and Benson felt his unemployment keenly. By October 1903, in order to move things along a little, Benson asked Esher to organise a visit to the Round Tower at Windsor Castle, where many of the papers were housed. From his first visit he was fascinated. Already it looked to be 'an enormous collection' but he was dismayed to see 'a great deal of German'. He was instantly seduced by the sentimental and historical associations of the material – 'Fancy all the love letters to the Prince Consort in one volume' – and by the setting of the Round Tower. On this same visit he and Esher chose workrooms and furniture, and then Esher took Benson to see the Prince Consort's bedroom – 'all his things – uniforms, walking sticks, the bed he died in; which the Queen kept in a room next to her own, which no one else visited. A strange mausoleum ... even the palms laid on his coffin, and casts of his hand and foot ...' Benson felt a new connection to the task following this visit: 'I hope and pray that I may be allowed to do the work there and do it well ... and that I may be serene and patient.' His prayer for patience was needed – he was delayed from starting work for four more months, and he did not bear the interlude well.

During this time Benson was invited to several social events at Windsor Castle and was occasionally 'summoned' for meetings with Esher. Although he was pleased when Esher greeted him as 'Dear Colleague', he was sometimes incensed by Esher's superior manner. After one such visit, he railed in his diary, 'I am not, by the way, going to pose as the humble hack – only let me get my foot in ...' He then described his long wait for Esher. While he waited, in the company of the adolescent Maurice, Benson had taken the opportunity to discuss the book with the biographer Fritz Ponsonby (son of Sir Henry Ponsonby, Victoria's longest serving private secretary; Fritz had lived most of his life in Windsor Castle) and Lord Knollys, the King's secretary. Esher later cautioned Benson not to discuss the project with anybody without his permission. 'I don't quite understand the politics of this visit,' Benson mused – but he was becoming aware of Esher's propensity for power-play.

While he waited for the work to begin, Benson read widely on the nineteenth century and met with other scholars and writers. He also recruited staff to assist with the editing. He hired Miss Bertha Williams, whom he quaintly referred to as 'the typewriter', who could copy 'from 6,000–10,000 words a day' and would 'give us all her time for £100 for the year'. She was, he told Esher, 'good at copying really difficult work and moreover is quite discreet'. This estimate of her speed, whether made by Benson or by Miss Williams herself, sounds optimistic, given she would have to decipher the handwriting and idiosyncratic expressions of multiple people, from letters held in tightly bound volumes.

Dr Eugene Oswald was hired as a researcher. After Benson's first meeting with Oswald, he reported to Esher that although he found Oswald to be 'discreet, cautious and competent ... I think he is rather an old slow-coach. However, I will spur him on.' A fortnight later he wrote in his diary, 'Dr O. is my bugbear just now. What I want is a <u>rapid</u> searcher who will frisk out a few salient extracts; but he goes fumbling along.' Later, Benson found he needed more particular assistance: for German and French translations he consulted two experts, Mr C.C. Perry and Mr G. Hua, and to check all the '<u>historical</u> statements' he chose a 'shining light of Modern History at Cambridge', J.W. Headlam. Each of these appointments had ultimately to be authorised by the King.

In February 1904, Benson visited Esher in London, hoping to get the work underway. They decided the thing to do was 'simply to attack the papers and find out what they are'. The next day, Benson was taken to Windsor and given a key to the 'strong room'. Work was finally to begin. Neither Benson nor Esher, however, recorded any firm decisions concerning topics to be included or excluded.

Over the first days, Benson's spirit dipped and soared. He began to regret accepting the job, lamenting that he was now 'more tied down than ever'. Benson was given to hypochondria and disliked uncertainty and lack of routine. In anticipation of hard work, he had taken a holiday in Cambridge after Christmas before coming to Windsor; when he found he was unable to begin, he was downcast. 'I am (not unnaturally) rather depressed & miserable just now ... I want to get settled into regular ways ... I seem to have no end of small ailments.' Three days later his enthusiasm was restored. He went to the castle and found that his room had been prepared for him. He was captivated by the 'quaint' interior of the Tower:

> ... odd passages with oak arches and an area of open space in the centre ... My own room is a big room hung with Hogarth engravings and good furniture – a white chair with pink satin on wheels was used by the Queen. I did not use [the room] today as it was not ready, but worked in the strong room and went through an interesting volume of Melbourne's letters – beginning with one on the morning of the Accession. His writing is very hard to read. It was odd to sit in this big room, all surrounded with shelves, with the deep embrasure filled with ferns ... The wind roared and the rain lashed the windows. I was amused and happy.

Although the next day was Saturday, he hurried back to read more of Melbourne's letters. However, Sunday brought

a very bad hour of despair on waking, about the book. I had roughly catalogued the volumes on Saturday and found that there were about 460! and out of this we are to make quite a little book. *Que faire!* And how am I to know what is interesting and what is not – However my course is at present: to go ploughing on with the papers & then decide.

Benson found himself enjoying the view from the Tower, especially of the Long Walk with its row of elms, and he sketched it in his diary. He even felt that he began to 'see the light – to issue a volume at a time, and to cut out a definite subject. It is the thing to do. Hope returns.'

Benson's mood swings – from confusion to despair and then resolve – were in direct contrast to Esher's steady character. Benson's resolutions frequently had little chance of success, being ill formed and premature, and therefore doomed to lead to further despair. Throughout the editing process, Benson would 'get a rush of blood,' confident that the task was nearing completion, only to be confronted with some new obstacle. Bundles and boxes of previously unknown letters would surface from other collections in the Royal Library, or from a distant room of the castle.

His domestic life did not help his mood. Benson was lodging at Mustians, the home of A.C. Ainger in nearby Eton. Ainger had tutored Esher at Eton and remained a guide and mentor throughout Esher's adult life; in the 1880s and 1890s, Esher's two sons had lived at Mustians, when they started at Eton. Here, billiards rather than conversation occupied the evenings. Benson hated billiards. And he had 'the strange experience of mingling with old friends who were no longer colleagues, of meeting daily boys over whom he no longer had any responsibility, and of living the life of a revenant ...' As February progressed, he felt much worse: 'I have not had such an acute attack of depression since I was at Cambridge, in 1882. It dogs me all day – though I can work and read it is all without savour or intellect.' He sadly described his condition as a 'neuralgia of the soul'.

As the month went on, however, Benson was relieved to be able to record something resembling a daily routine:

> I get to the Castle by 10.30 and I am let in by one of my faithful henchmen. It astonishes me to find how <u>pleasant</u> the Castle servants all are. Then I go to the Strong room to select a few volumes for upstairs; see what Miss Williams is doing: and then begin work. I write a letter or two, and then just read and select. The work is very interesting and time flies past ... lunch ... walk ... tea at 5.00, work till 8.00 reading and writing. I suppose I do about 6 hours work a day, but very concentrated work. I see a glimmer of light with regard to the book now. One must have a brief introduction & plunge into the letters at once – There is certainly no lack – & plenty of good footnotes must be appended to explain people. I have written a sketch of much of my Introduction already.

On finding how many volumes of letters were to be gone through, Benson soon realised that he would need an assistant. Esher suggested that a soldier might be suitable. Instead, Benson's old Eton friend, Hugh Childers, offered to do the job for £100 per year and to be at Windsor four days per week. Childers was 'a good worker' and knew political history well. He was the son of H.C. Childers, a politician who had begun his career in Australia before returning to take up a seat in Westminster. In the editorial note to the first published volume, Hugh Childers is recognised for his 'ungrudging help in the preparation of the Introductory annual summaries, and in the political and historical annotation, as well as for his invaluable co-operation at every stage of the work'. He also supported Benson as a friend and they holidayed together in 1905.

It is possible that in suggesting a soldier for the position of assistant, Esher was hoping to have Maurice appointed. By this time, Maurice had served in the Coldstream Guards for nearly two years, during which time his father had pulled 'every string for his advancement' while still obsessively seeking out his company. Esher had an inflated view of Maurice's abilities (Benson described Maurice as 'stolid and rosy'). Considering the range of tasks undertaken by Childers, had Maurice been Benson's assistant, the book might never have been published. The tone of the editors' correspondence on this issue suggests some coolness, although Esher later complimented Benson on Childers' work.

Benson agonised over the working conditions for his staff. He worried that some of the rooms were too dark for long hours of reading. There were logistical problems concerning keys and access to the Round Tower. On one occasion, he found himself locked in and had 'a ten minute walk around the whole Castle' in order to find someone to let him out. Further, there were major interruptions to the work when the King visited Windsor, as the editors' workrooms were required to accommodate the King's retinue. Benson was relieved, however, that the work was at last underway. 'I hear the typewriter clicking next door,' he reported with satisfaction.

As there was no single repository for royal papers, aside from the limited storage space in the Royal Library (there was no Royal Archive yet) and the strong room, Benson and Esher soon realised that accurately ascertaining what material was available was going to be difficult. In addition to the 460 volumes that Benson had 'roughly catalogued' on that first day, additional boxes of letters were continually 'being turned up'. Benson reported to Esher that Mr Vaughan, the library bookbinder, found letters from Queen Victoria's eldest daughter, Empress Frederick, in a box on the landing by his window; other boxes were discovered in a stone vault under the Grand Staircase in the Upper Ward of Windsor Castle, a building adjacent to the Round Tower. More letters from Victoria's uncle, King Leopold I of the Belgians, arrived just as Benson was getting the first batch straight, which was 'rather a ghastly business'. 'Are there any more papers among those which came out of the Library which concern us?' he asked Esher. The problem was so acute that by the first week of March 1904, Benson conceded, 'I am very grateful now the King vetoed applying for <u>private</u> papers'; the documents already in royal possession would keep them busy enough.

In these early days, the editors decided to ignore 'a very large series of volumes entitled GERMANY, which we decided would be foreign to our purpose', and, rather strangely, the papers of the Prince Consort. Later Benson had second thoughts and 'glanced through 2 or 3 volumes and found some very important and interesting things … so I am working through them'. Following this discovery, Benson suggested to Esher that although it would cause some delay, they must also go through Albert's papers, 'as it seems he annexed drafts and letters [of Queen Victoria's corre-spondence] for his collection'. Both editors admired Prince Albert's 'industry and intelligence'. There is no evidence that they ever requested materials from other archives or European courts or that they even thought of doing so. They were Englishmen, and did not recognise the extent to which Victoria had been a European.

Accessing materials could be difficult. Vaughan, as well as being the bookbinder, was the custodian of the keys to various locked volumes of letters, and would only hand them over to Benson on Esher's express orders. Benson had to ask Esher to intervene with the 'incorruptible Vaughan' on sev-eral occasions. For example:

> Would you kindly authorise Vaughan to let me have the series of the Queen's letters to the King of the Belgians, of which I already have 7 vols? … Also would you instruct him just to see that there are no papers dating back ear-lier than 1844. We shall soon have the material made up; and it would be a bore if a new lot were to be plumped on the scales!

After the letters were located, they were catalogued, and then Benson made his selections. These selections were typed, or 'copied' as Benson called it, and assembled into chronological order. From these typed copies Benson, and later Childers, had to identify the individuals mentioned and contextualise the contents in order to judge their signif-icance. Benson then made further selections and excisions, and the letters were retyped and sent to Esher for further editing. Benson agreed that he would then 'go through the whole thing again very carefully and follow your [Esher's] directions' before the letters were retyped and sent to John Murray for printing. (This constant retyping was necessary to ensure that no material deemed unsuitable for publication was seen by the publisher or by the humble typesetters.)

When there were French or German passages or phrases to be translated, Benson asked Mr Hua to verify phrases in the proofs. Esher forcefully directed Benson that the proofs must not be given to Hua without his approval. This was impractical and probably unnecessarily cautious given that Hua had impeccable credentials. He had previously been employed by the Royal family to instruct the two sons of the Prince of Wales, Princes Eddy and George (later King George V), in French, and in 1883 he had accompanied them on a trip to France and Switzerland. Further, until the passages were translated, neither Benson nor Esher could judge their meaning or their value.

The typeset proofs were later made available to John Morley (biographer of Gladstone and later 1st Viscount Morley of Blackburn) and to Arthur Bigge (private secretary to Queen Victoria, later Lord Stamfordham), in preparation for the King's eye and a final edit before publication.

Throughout this process, Benson, Esher and John Murray referred to the whole project, comprising three volumes, as 'the book'. The general time frame (1837–61, from Victoria's accession to the throne to Albert's death) was established from the start, but the exact scope of each volume was altered several times. In the end, Volume I began with an introductory section on the origins of the Houses of Hanover and Coburg and details of Victoria's early life and family, followed by selections of correspondence from 1821 to 1843; Volume II contained correspondence from 1844 to 1853; and Volume III 1854 to 1861.

A major constraint, one which had to be determined as early as possible, was the space available. In the early stages, Benson sent some sample letters to John Murray to be typeset and printed, in order to ascertain how much room they would occupy as a guide to further editing. In March 1904, an introductory passage and letters up to May 1838 (that is, only ten months in to the 24-year range of the book) were estimated to take up 357 pages, which was 'in great excess of our space'. In the final published work, May 1838 is reached by page 113 of Volume I, which means further editing reduced the selection by almost 70 per cent.

There were also decisions to be made about the page setting, including the size and choice of typeface. Murray sent specimens for Benson and Esher to look over, including some samples from his recent edition of *The Creevey Papers*, a selection of the letters and diaries of Thomas Creevey, an English politician of the early nineteenth century. The 'small print of the Creevey page was not at all agreeable,' Benson complained to Esher.

Then there were footnotes and an index to consider. Most of the notes were prepared by Hugh Childers; he also contributed some of the introductory passages outlining the major political events of each year; Benson referred to this material, borrowing from Kant, as the 'Prolegomena'. Benson wanted to submit this introductory material to J.W. Headlam at Cambridge for his opinion. When Esher expressed surprise at the suggestion, Benson placated him, somewhat tongue in cheek: 'It is essential that this part should be <u>impeccable</u>, and I have therefore arranged that he should criticise ... such an arrangement is necessary, even for such gifted amateurs as ourselves!' Esher and Knollys became anxious whenever 'outsiders' were given any access to royal material.

In preparing these explanatory notes, Childers drew heavily on his own political knowledge and on the networks of Benson and Esher. Trying to ascertain the identity of people mentioned in the letters, as well as the senders and recipients, was often difficult, given so many Christian names were used repeatedly among cousins and down the generations. Making sense of these personages was an essential step; without it, the editors, the King and eventually the book's readers would have no way of knowing whether a letter was important, irrelevant, or potentially scandalous.

The *dramatis personae* of the letters comprised an immense assembly. Victoria lived for eighty-one years, from 1819 until 1901. She corresponded with (and about) other members of the royal family, courtiers and aristocrats, as well as politicians, churchmen and representatives of the military, the universities and the arts; there were letters from manufacturers and magnates, Chartists, Lords and the lowliest villagers; and there were many letters from female relatives, friends, aristocrats and colonials. Even though the book would only include letters written before the death of the Prince Consort in December 1861, older and more recent history still had to be considered: the letters referred to members of earlier generations, and the sensitivities of their descendants also had to be taken into account. Benson and Esher therefore needed a thorough knowledge of who was who.

Sometimes, however, identifying her correspondents proved impossible. Although Victoria and Albert were first cousins and shared one branch of their family tree, that of the Saxe-Coburgs, there had been seven children in their parents' generation, all of whom married and produced children. On Victoria's Hanoverian side, her grandfather, King

George III, had fifteen children, five of whom had produced legitimate offspring. There were also many illegitimate off-spring, some of whom had been given positions at court and in the army and hence needed to be identified by the editors. Although Victoria herself had an encyclopaedic knowledge of her own and others' genealogy, it soon became apparent that few members of the royal family in 1905 knew the names of their many great-uncles and great-aunts, or their numerous descendants. Childers consulted the College of Arms with some success: his visit led to an up-to-date Royal Pedigree being compiled. Several times he went to great lengths to ascertain the identity of someone named in Victoria's corre-spondence, only to discover that the name referred to a pet!

There were also to be illustrations, prepared by John Murray's brother, Hallam. Planning for these began simul-taneously with the editing. As early as March 1904, Benson and Hallam drew up an 'exhaustive list of all possible illus-trations for Vol. 1 – people mentioned in letters &c &c'. Hal-lam was keen to have photographs made of portraits of these people promptly, as he was exploring various new technologies for their reproduction. He was particularly interested in a new method of producing plates that would maintain the quality of the reproduction over a print run of five thousand copies. Benson wrote to Esher:

> Saw Hallam Murray … He showed me some new copper-plates, by a new process. He is going very carefully into the question as to whether it will be well to use it. It is much more expeditious & much less expensive than the old – and the pictures he showed me are <u>admirable</u>. He is going however to get more specimens, & I will submit them to you …

71

In his diary for the same day, Benson was more exuberant:

> Hallam showed me a new copperplate process. It has
> always before needed to be inked and pressed <u>by hand</u>.
> This does it by machinery. He told me that if they would
> adopt it, it would save <u>£4000</u> in this book alone!!! That
> shows what a scale we shall work on ...

The men were all impressed by the various tints that
were becoming available, ranging from 'old browns' to
'warm browns' to 'hotter browns'. In a climate of rapid tech-
nological development, the possibilities seemed endless.

Selecting the illustrations brought more trouble for Benson. After consulting Esher, he sent a list of possible subjects
to Lionel Cust, keeper of the King's pictures and director of
the National Portrait Gallery, asking his advice as to 'which
were the best pictures'. He would then need to seek the
King's permission to have the portraits photographed.
Unbeknown to Benson, however, Hallam Murray had
already asked Cust if Benson might be admitted to Buckingham Palace to view some portraits in the King's private sitting rooms. Cust asked Lord Knollys, the King's secretary.
Knollys 'consents, not very graciously,' Benson recorded in
his diary; protocols had been upset. Trying to smooth things
over, Benson wrote to Esher:

> Cust is very anxious that he should not be thought to have
> interfered. As matters stand he is at present engaged to
> take me to Buckingham Palace some day soon at 10 a.m.
> ... Will you put this right on Monday? There is no necessity
> to visit Buckingham Palace in this solemn way, as if we
> were going to value for probate.

Meanwhile Knollys complained to Esher about 'Cust's interference' and Esher summoned Benson to his room, insinuating that the King was annoyed. Esher referred waspishly to Cust as an 'awful meddler, always asking for things' and offered Benson some advice: '"No greater mistake," said E. smiling, "than to ask for anything in this world unless you are nearly sure to get it."' Whereupon Benson was at pains to distance himself from Cust's inept assertiveness.

In an elegant display of power and *savoir faire,* Esher then airily conducted Benson down to the King's private rooms 'to see what pictures there were …' Benson soon forgot his discomfiture and was captivated:

> There are some lovely things. There is a little <u>audience chamber</u> of QV's fitted up so by Prince Albert with pictures and miniatures – very Victorian but such treasures. A row of heads of George III's children by Gainsborough. So strange to see those fussy, absurd, big, voluble men as graceful boys with low collars. The Dukes of Cambridge and Sussex are simply charming. Then to the Queen's rooms – such exquisite things and to the King's room where there is a Winterhalter of Queen Victoria with an unbound tress of hair – such a touching, *intime* thing – and a ludicrous Landseer where Prince Albert sits in a drawing room in shooting clothes, with the ribbon of the Garter and a table covered with hares, ducks and kingfishers. It is high day, but the Queen stands beside him dressed for dinner.

Before this visit, Benson knew the Queen as a little old lady in her widow's weeds and deep black bonnet. He had probably seen very few, if any, pictures of her as a young woman. The Winterhalter painting he described was a beguiling portrait of the young Queen with her hair down and her head tilted back, exposing her bare neck and shoulders. It was commissioned by Victoria as a surprise birthday present for Albert in 1843, in the fourth year of their marriage. It was significant that Benson saw these very intimate portraits so early on in the editing.

After this meeting with Esher, Benson lamented in his diary that he had managed to 'fall foul' of the King 'thrice times already'. Poor Benson! The King almost certainly knew nothing of his offences. Esher and Knollys, both experienced courtiers, artfully ensured that those around them were permanently anxious about Court protocol. That evening, in a bid to recover face, Benson concluded his diary with: 'Wrote a snappish note to Cust ...'

Chapter 5

THE EDITING

BENSON WAS ASTOUNDED AT the rapidity with which Esher did his editorial work. One Friday afternoon about eight weeks into the editing, Esher came to collect 'all of their work to date'. Benson's diary entry conveyed some resentment:

> Went up to the Castle & got there very hot. Esher came in as if he had nothing in the world to do – cool, graceful, charming. I showed him our materials and he carried it all off in a tin box. What a luxury to have had none of the work of selecting &c but to read all this interesting stuff through merely excising and omitting. He is a very fortunate prince!

The following Monday, Benson returned to the Castle and found that Esher had already returned the box. Benson was flabbergasted! When he looked over Esher's corrections, he made the first of many gentle protests to his editor-in-chief: 'I quite agree with your suggestions except in one or two very minute points. There should be a little spice of triviality I think preserved to give a hint of humanity. This applies to about three harmless excisions …'

Esher seems to have responded that the excisions were far from 'harmless', and to have suggested that they were based on the King's own objections. 'Why has H.M. become alarmed?' Benson asked. 'Has anyone been talking? There is plenty to omit, but I don't want it to become a colourless and official book. That would be losing a great opportunity.' Esher was much more cautious, and Benson already felt a certain vexation on this point. He recorded in his diary: 'The King seems to have taken fright, according to Esher, [and] has been cautioning him that there is to be nothing private, nothing scandalous, nothing *intime*, nothing malicious.' If there had been a more formal set of guidelines, perhaps the King's anxieties could have been more easily assuaged. But his concerns about scandal and malice continued, as did those of Esher. The following weekend, Esher visited Benson:

> [Esher] said that he must warn me once more, & I must warn Childers against any indiscretion – that we had better not say anything even about having seen private papers – speak of State Documents only. He thinks the King nervous and fussy about it all. I expect someone has been talking. He says he has not told the King how private some of the papers are. I was able to reassure E. on that point. I said, 'They are <u>private</u> – but they are not <u>confidential</u> exactly as a rule – there is <u>nothing</u> of which, if I were an unscrupulous man I can [sic] make any use of to exploit blackmail.'

Only a few days earlier, Benson had assured Esher, 'There is no difficulty about <u>scandal</u>. I can honestly say that that element has been rigidly excluded in my selections.' He added, most perceptively: 'As to ill-natured references, it is of course a more difficult matter because there are certain people who consider everything ill-natured that is not adulatory, when applied to deceased persons.'

Meanwhile the editing proceeded. Benson frequently employed agricultural metaphors to describe his work: 'ploughing'; 'hewing'; 'slashing and hacking'; 'bright sun, westerly wind worked at Castle … I worked savagely, cutting like a backwoodsman.'

The editors had no agreed plan for the book or the principles of selection when they began. The format was based on the traditional 'Life and Letters' biographies that had become so popular in the nineteenth century, some of which had been published by John Murray. A compilation of letters and autobiographical fragments, intended to allow the subject to speak for him or herself, was deemed the purest form of biography. This was what Esher had in mind. Unfortunately, as a genre, it had come to consist of expansive, multi-volume productions such as the one Queen Victoria commissioned to commemorate the life of the Prince Consort. Although it was written by Theodore Martin, the historian Walter Arnstein has suggested that Victoria contributed substantially to it. Benson criticised it as too long and almost unreadable, yet it set the standard for such biographies. The genre was later pilloried by Lytton Strachey, who lamented

> those two fat volumes with which it is our custom to commemorate the dead – Who does not know them, with their ill-digested masses of material, their slipshod style, their tone of tedious panegyric, their lamentable lack of selection, of detachment, of design? They are as familiar as the *cortège* of the undertaker and wear the same air of slow,

funereal barbarism. One is tempted to suppose, of some
of them, that they are composed by that functionary, as
the final item of his job.

Virginia Woolf later complained that the subjects of such
works appeared 'very much overworked, very serious, very
joyless'. Since such books relied chiefly on important – usually serious – documents, they could be rather colourless.
The notion that they allowed the subject to speak for herself
was also problematic. Not all the documents were in her
voice – often they were letters to her by others, mostly men.
But even when the 'voice' belonged to the subject, in this
case the Queen, her words were being selected and edited,
and from an already restricted collection – that is, from the
surviving written records.

Benson and Esher wanted to avoid the stigma associated
with such stiff and bloated volumes. In keeping with the
ideas of the time, however, they considered that the historical facts, set out chronologically, should dictate the shape
and tone of their book. In following this convention, Queen
Victoria's childhood and genealogy were compressed into
seventy-one pages. The following twenty-four years, from
her accession in 1837 until Albert's death in 1861, occupied
the bulk of the remaining fifteen hundred pages.

The original idea, as discussed by Esher and Benson, was
to publish two or perhaps three volumes. When John Murray
was consulted, he agreed, adding that, 'the materials should
afford a general guide and be allowed to shape themselves …
to the best advantage'. Two or three volumes would be readable by a general audience and hence marketable and, as
Benson said frequently: 'I so want the book to be read!'

Benson constantly agonised over the material being

excluded and whether the book should be expanded. When he made his first visit to the Round Tower and counted over four hundred volumes of bound material, two or three volumes immediately seemed too limiting; he knew that much interesting material would have to be rejected. The more he read, the more he despaired at the space constraints. After reading King Leopold's correspondence with the Queen for the first time, he described it as 'a tremendous acquisition – I really think that if I had been *au fait* with the whole thing I should have <u>simply</u> advised the publication of [this] correspondence … It quite goes to my heart to dock it.' Esher wrote to Lord Knollys (but not to Benson) expressing the same anxiety, but he was still hopeful that the selection could be 'compressed' into three volumes.

As he worked away at the Windsor coalface, Benson felt impelled to submit an argument for four volumes. Just two months after commencing work, he wrote to Esher:

My dear Esher,

… It will be a real disaster if the book is curtailed. I think it <u>could</u> be done in four volumes; but you will remember that [at the outset] I was very strong for two volumes. Since I have seen the collection I feel quite differently. I have no doubt that the interest aroused by the book will be very great indeed, and I think it can be averred that for each volume we produce, at least two could be produced without any diminution of interest.

It might be respectfully submitted to His Majesty

1. That the interest of the book to a great extent depends upon the additional and vivid detail which it gives the historical and social events and the sidelights which it throws. To truncate the letters too much or to

omit letters will be to deprive these episodes of much of their interest. One can't omit the important letters; but the events narrated by them are not always familiar, and it is by taking the letters all together that the interest of the book will be produced.

2. By producing the book volume by volume the grave objection to the 4-volume form is removed. People would find a 4 volume book, all of which appeared simultaneously, rather too solid, it is true – but not when the volumes came out one by one. I will answer for it that no reader of volume one, will be disappointed, or will not look forward with anything but intense interest to volume two.

3. It must be remembered that the letters are not like <u>literary</u> letters, where the style is the main attraction – the simplicity, the frankness, the good sense of many of these letters are a great charm – but the wide range of affairs and the inner knowledge of politics are the great points – & such characteristics can only be brought out by full reflections.

If the smaller number of volumes is <u>decided</u> upon, the only way will be to give up any idea of [the correspondence giving] a connected history of the years – if that were done in 2 volumes, the letters would merely be a few frigid extracts – & we must instead just choose a few episodes arbitrarily and give them in full.

It must be remembered that this is after all biographical <u>material</u>. If such a book as the *Life of Mr Gladstone* takes three volumes, what would an issue of illustrative letters have occupied.

One other point – as it stands the letters to a great extent form their own comment; but if the book is made a short one, long introduction & notes will be absolutely necessary to explain the letters – & this in my opinion would be wholly a mistake. My idea is that we should efface ourselves as much as possible, only just giving enough explanation & comment for an ordinary reader to understand.

This letter needs no immediate answer. But please let me know as soon as possible what is decided ... In fact I simply don't think it <u>can</u> be done more briefly, though I quite appreciate the advisability of brevity.

Ever yours,

A.C.B.

Benson was overwhelmed again and again by the size of the archive and what they were trying to achieve. His focus at this stage seems to have been the 'historical and social events' in which Victoria had participated as a public figure. He does not seem to have been particularly interested in Victoria 'the woman', or even Victoria 'the person'. Esher began the project from a much more pragmatic and political standpoint – the need for a memorial, but not of monumental proportions. Initially he thought, or hoped, that two volumes would suffice, and was reluctant to consider more than one additional volume.

Benson, in his usual manner, continued to waver. In January 1905, when the material for Volume I sent to Murray amounted to about sixteen hundred pages and Benson calculated that at least a third of it would need to be cut, his initial solution was again to consider a fourth volume. He went on, however, 'I am myself strongly against this. The book will then become a standard work, a work of reference not a book to be read ...' Six months later, he mentioned the possibility again; a prodigious amount of cutting was still necessary, he lamented, 'unless we do run to four vols'. Every time a new stash of letters was found, Benson despaired of having to cut still further: 'vol iii must be reduced – by throwing out whole episodes, not by simply starving episodes or omitting detail ...' Again and again, he questioned the decision to opt for three volumes rather than four or even five!

Such vacillation may have been a source of annoyance and frustration to Esher. On 2 August 1905, and again on 5 August, Benson reiterated his view that it would be impossible to condense the remaining material into Volume III, and again suggested a fourth volume. When Esher did not reply, Benson wrote directly to the King on 9 August, asking for a fourth volume. Lord Knollys alerted Esher to Benson's request, writing:

> It is evident from Benson's letter that if there are only three [volumes] much matter of interest will have to be omitted and this H.M. thinks would be a pity ... I think the King was shaken about by Benson – I don't however think he [the King] has any strong views on the subject, and if you saw him, I have no doubt you would bring him over to your way of thinking – at the same time – if you do not consider that 4 volumes will be actually injurious to the sale of the work perhaps it had better be four, unless you like to wait and go through the material again.

Lord Esher replied, setting out quite simply his view for the book:

> I want the letters to tell their own story.
> This they do.

They exhibit:

(a) the early training of the Queen by Melbourne and Peel

(b) the 'coming of the Prince Consort'

(c) the influence over him of the King of the Belgians and Stockmar

(d) the growth of their [the Queen's and Prince's] powers

(e) the change in the relations of the Crown to the Ministers after the retirement of Aberdeen [January 1855]

(f) the culmination of the Prince Consort's rule 1859–1861.

This list in effect summarises the first edition of the book as it eventually appeared, giving a slender narrative outline of her life that differed very little from that used by Sidney Lee in his entry for the *Dictionary of National Biography* and the biography he published in 1902. This narrative focused on the men who surrounded the Queen, and this was the template that made sense to Benson and Esher. (As we shall see, the unpublished letters exhibited many other things.)

Knollys replied to Esher:

If Benson is only inclined to have 4 Vols in order to insert short biographical sketches and accounts of political questions, I more than agree with you that there should only be three. Cannot you write me a letter which I can forward to the King of the same purport as that which you have sent to me. I feel pretty sure that if you give the reasons which induce Benson to wish for 4 Vols as you have done to me, that H.M. will come into agreement with you on the subject.

Esher, being a master polemicist, did not put Benson's

arguments quite accurately to Knollys. Benson's earlier point had not been that he *wanted* to provide 'short biographical sketches and accounts of political questions', but that if only short excerpts from the letters were included, more extensive explanatory notes would be required.

Three days later, Esher took Knollys's advice and wrote to the King, attaching a copy of the letter he had written to Benson. He reiterated to the King that it would still be possible 'to get into three volumes everything which is necessary towards exhibiting in its fullness, the development of the Queen's character between 1837–1861, as well as the working of the Monarchical system under the Queen and the Prince Consort.' A reply came from Marienbad, Austria, where the King had gone to take the waters, saying that His Majesty 'thinks three volumes should meet the case and be preferable to four'. The message was conveyed to Benson, who recorded in his diary: 'The King decides for 3 vols. This is a relief!' Yet Benson was to raise the issue several more times before the book was published. When another collection of correspondence between Queen Victoria and Lord Melbourne surfaced in January 1906, he asked: 'I suppose it will not involve a fourth volume?' And when more letters from Lord John Russell were found in May, he was hugely exasperated. He requested that a note be inserted in the preface, stating that the correspondence was found too late to be included.

This ongoing debate about the number of volumes had one positive outcome. In order to convince both Benson and the King of the strength of his opinion and his command over the project, Esher finally set down the parameters for the book in its entirety, elaborating on the summary he had sent to Knollys. On 20 August 1905 he wrote:

My dear A.C.B.,

I quite realize the difficulties, but I am SURE that we shall do wisely to stick to three volumes.

The great thing is to get in our minds what we want to do. The main object, almost the sole object, is to exhibit the true relation between the character of the Queen and the government of her people.

(a) the formation of her character

(b) the early experience of power

(c) her schooling in the art of government

   (1) Melbourne

   (2) King Leopold

   (3) Prince Consort

(d) her method of government

(e) her sense of 'Kingship'

(f) her motherly view of her people

(g) her guiding principles

(h) the controlling Power of the Sovereign

It is impossible for us to give full accounts of political and historical episodes and personages. They come in partly as

(a) illustrations

(b) scenery and *dramatis personae*

The central figure moving through it all is that of the Queen herself.

All of the work in these three volumes is preparatory, to the other volumes which some day will follow – WHEN THE QUEEN IS ALONE.

The book must be dramatic, or rather possess a dramatic note. If we keep these main ideas in view, (and if you agree with them), all cutting must be subordinate to them.

I am roughly working along these lines. Of course I
am making mistakes, but we can correct them together.

Yours ever,

Esher

Esher thus set out his goals for the project in a form that
would both appeal to the King and be persuasive of Benson.
Before he did so, however, eighteen months of selecting,
rejecting, incorporating and cutting had already taken
place. It is impossible to ascertain whether Esher was simply
restating previous decisions or whether it was the first time
he had conceptualised the parameters so clearly. He also
wrote with conspiratorial bravado to Knollys, 'As you say,
Arthur Benson is undecided as to what the general purpose
of the book is to be. I am quite clear that it <u>ought</u> to be what
I have said ...' Even so, Esher made a copy of his letter for
his own records, something he rarely did. (He retained and
filed thousands of letters, but very few letters written by him
are in his archive.) Esher clearly attached great significance
to this document.

Benson was pleased to have such a succinct summary of
the book. He replied:

3 vols!!

Your analysis of the object of the book is masterly; I will, if
I may, embody your points in the introduction. I wholly
and entirely concur, ... but to aim at bringing out <u>her
character</u> and not illustrating history that is the exact aim.
When I go through the second vol again, which I shall do
in the next few days, I shall ask myself not 'Is this important?' but 'Is this characteristic?'

At the same time, as you say, <u>it must be dramatic</u>.

Esher had given Benson a useful framework, a checklist against which he could judge the relevance of each letter and justify its inclusion or excision. By now, the two editors had come a long way from allowing the Queen to speak for herself. Most 'Life and Letters' biographies were, as Strachey complained, shapeless. But if they contained all or most of the subject's letters, readers could at least form their own opinions. The Queen's correspondence, however, was so immense that the editors had now decided firmly against shapeless comprehensiveness: the book was to tell a dramatic story, the shape and significance of which they would determine.

PART II

THE QUEEN

NOT TO GIVE OFFENCE AND NOT TO CREATE scandal, but to make each of the three volumes of the book dramatic: these were the aims of the editors. Episodes which might have added drama to the book were sacrificed in order to avoid scandal and the King's displeasure. Benson grasped this dilemma early in the process: 'We are between the devil and the deep blue sea. The King will be furious if we violate confidence, and displeased if the book is dull.' The task was made even more difficult because they were not dealing with the authoritative, older woman they had both known; instead they had to portray a much younger Victoria, in her first forty-two years.

Benson and Esher generated drama by producing a romantic idealisation of Victoria's life – of a young girl, pure, petite and innocent, under some duress; then her awakening as she flowered as a constitutional monarch, under the fortunate tutelage of particular and gifted gentlemen. To highlight this process, they portrayed Victoria's girlhood as one of feminine isolation. Her queenship they depicted as one of youthful vitality and a keenness to learn from older men, especially from Lord Melbourne, the Prime Minister of the first years of her reign. In this narrative, the throne brought liberation from her mother's control, but this independence was soon overtaken by marriage and a husband's influence. Victoria's correspondence with other women was omitted, Benson said, to avoid triviality. Her European correspondence was minimised in order to avoid suggesting undue foreign influence. There was little mention of her children.

And so the image of the Queen that emerged was shaped by a series of factors: by the documents that survived and were readily available; by omissions resulting from loss, oversight or rejection; and then by further excisions and deletions as the editing proceeded.

Chapter 6

Sir John Conroy and the Ghost of Lady Flora

Victoria's father, Edward, Duke of Kent, had died suddenly when she was eight months old. On his deathbed he had asked his equerry, John Conroy, to care for his widow and child. The Duchess of Kent had very limited English and even more limited funds. Her husband left her with an income of £6000 per year and debts of £50,000. Her brother Leopold, later to be named King of the Belgians, provided her with some financial assistance and her brother-in-law, King George IV, allowed her to keep some of her husband's rooms at Kensington Palace. The Conroy family lived nearby and the children played frequently with Victoria.

John Conroy was a very ambitious man. He later came to be comptroller of the affairs of Victoria's two unmarried aunts, who also lived at Kensington Palace. As Victoria moved closer to the throne, he insinuated himself further into her mother's affairs. Conroy sought to direct Victoria's education and began to suggest that she had various infirmities that would preclude her ruling alone. He organised tours through the provinces to 'show her to the people'; she was made to stand on platforms and podiums but, as was the custom of the day, was not allowed to say anything. Many years later, in a letter to Lord John Russell, she vividly described her abhorrence of being 'a spectacle' to be 'gazed at, without delicacy or feeling'. Being 'on display' was something Victoria would dislike for the rest of her life. When her older half-sister, Feodore (her mother's daughter from her first marriage), left England to marry the Prince of Hohenlohe-Langenburg, Victoria – then nine years old – became even more isolated and came to rely on her governess, Louise Lehzen, for company and support.

The division within the household increased when Lady Flora Hastings became the Duchess of Kent's Lady of the Bedchamber. Lady Flora colluded with Conroy and the Duchess to enforce what came to be known as the 'Kensington System'. This strict program for the Princess's education was designed to distance her from the Court, and became a vehicle for the political aspirations of the Duchess and of Conroy. Two factions now developed within the household: the Duchess and her allies versus Victoria and Lehzen. The factions were irrevocably established by the time Victoria was sixteen. While on holiday at Ramsgate that year, Victoria contracted an illness. Elizabeth Longford suggested that it was typhoid fever but other historians, such as Stanley Weintraub, have attributed it to the psychological warfare in the household. During this illness Conroy tried to persuade Victoria to sign a statement asking that her mother rule as regent until Victoria was twenty-one and guaranteeing that Conroy would be given the post of private secretary when she acceded the throne. With Lehzen's help Victoria resisted his bullying, but the episode remained with her. The steely resolve noted throughout her life was forged during this time.

The situation persisted for the next two years. In the months before Victoria's eighteenth birthday, her uncle King William IV offered financial help to establish her own household. In doing so, he may have hoped to relieve her of Conroy's influence. There is a series of letters between Queen Adelaide, Feodore and the Duchess of Northumberland (Victoria's official governess, a ceremonial role distinct from the day-to-day duties of Louise Lehzen) expressing their grave concerns for Victoria's mental and physical well-being. In 1836, Feodore hid a note to the Duchess of Northumberland in a letter to Queen Adelaide, which she sent in the care of a private citizen; she hoped to avoid it being intercepted by Conroy. In this note she urged the Duchess to try to ascertain Victoria's 'health and spirits'; she 'has suffered a good deal, as you will know ... her caracter [sic] might be completely spoiled by this continual warfare'.

By late 1836 or early 1837, Uncle Leopold in Belgium had also heard about the 'Kensington System'. He too began to discuss the logistics of creating a separate household for the Princess. But King William's health was deteriorating. Less than a month after Victoria's eighteenth birthday, he died and Victoria acceded the throne in her own right. Almost immediately, she moved decisively to isolate herself from her mother and from Conroy. Her handling of the delicate situation of Lady Flora Hastings showed how high tensions ran.

In 1838, Lady Flora developed an abdominal swelling which Queen Victoria and Lord Melbourne attributed to pregnancy. They cast their suspicions upon Conroy; Flora and Conroy were flirtatious with one another and had shared a long coach journey several months prior. As rumours flew around the court, Victoria's doctor, Sir James Clark, was consulted and Lady Flora was persuaded to agree to a medical examination. The exam confirmed that she was a virgin. The doctors were puzzled and met with Lord Melbourne, who passed their reports on to the Queen. Victoria told her mother that 'though [Flora] is a virgin ... there was an enlargement in the womb like a child'. Lady Flora's family criticised Victoria and Melbourne in the press for casting such scurrilous aspersions on Flora's reputation, and for subjecting a lady to the indignity of such an examination. Sadly Lady Flora died several months later from a liver tumour.

Readers in 1907 already had access to published accounts of these episodes. One such, to which Esher referred when he discussed the issue with Benson, was the diaries of Charles Greville. Edited by Henry Reeve, these were published in 1874 in three volumes; a second series was brought out in 1885. Greville was well known to Victoria as the clerk of the Privy Council from 1821–59 and as a leading figure in London society, and Victoria herself enjoyed his journals. Characteristically, she declared them to be 'very exaggerated' but nevertheless 'full of truth'.

In recounting the Flora Hastings affair, in a one-page entry dated 2 March 1839, Greville observed that 'it is not easy to ascertain what and how much is true'. He was critical of Lord Melbourne's role, accusing him of advising the Queen badly: 'It is inconceivable how Melbourne can have permitted this disgraceful and mischievous scandal,' he wrote. Flora Hastings does not appear again in the diaries until July, when Greville recorded her death. If Greville recorded the many other instalments in the affair that occurred in the intervening months, Reeve did not include them. In a footnote, Reeve apologised for including this 'painful transaction which had better be consigned to oblivion' but explained that he did so 'because it contains nothing which is not to be found in the most ordinary books of reference; but I shall not enter further on this matter'.

Not everyone blamed Lord Melbourne for the affair. In 1902, Sir Sidney Lee had published a biography of the Queen. He devoted three pages to the demise of Lady Flora and the subsequent public hostility towards Victoria. Citing the Greville memoirs as one of his sources, Lee declared them to be 'outspoken but in the main trustworthy'. He divided the blame for the Hastings affair between the Queen's 'youth and inexperience' and the malice of Lehzen, rather than Lord Melbourne.

Lee sent the recently crowned King Edward VII a copy of his *Queen Victoria* and Lord Knollys replied on the King's behalf: 'The King thanks Sir Sidney for the copy of the *Life of Queen Victoria*. He admires very much the binding of the volume. His Majesty feels sure that he shall read your history of the late reign with great interest.' The King probably never got past the binding. He was notoriously uninterested in reading and was utterly dismayed when Esher spoke to him of matters that were detailed in Lee's book. Esher reported to Benson:

the King was very <u>uncertain,</u> going backwards and forwards according to what the last person said. Sometimes utterly regretting that he had ever allowed the letters to be published. All the old scandals, the Duke of Kent's debts, the Conroy business, the Lady Flora Hastings business & so on – the King has never heard of them. He doesn't read memoirs & of course no one dares talk to him of such things – so that when he hears about them, or gathers that there is anything about them in the letters, he is first of all horribly concerned at the thought that even <u>you</u> should see them – and upset at the bare idea that ordinary people should read about them – it is no good telling him that everybody who knows anything knows far more about them than he does himself; & that they won't arouse comment simply because they are so stale ...

When Esher showed the King the letters relating to the Flora Hastings affair, the King was 'astonished at the precocious knowledge shown by the Queen [aged nineteen] and the outspokenness of Lord Melbourne'.

In March 1904, when Benson sent off the first instalment of the manuscript to John Murray, Murray admitted that he could not resist spending the evening reading through the selections from the Kensington period:

many of the letters are of the greatest importance. I am struck by some of those from the Queen to her mother. Her position was a most delicate one in regard to the Duchess of Kent both shortly before and after her Coronation, and these letters display much firmness of character and sense of justice.

Within two months, however, Benson was asking Murray to return these sections, as he had been directed by Esher that 'certain matters' had to be eliminated. Benson told Murray, 'I fear that the Duchess of Kent Correspondence will have to disappear – it seems to be a particularly sensitive point. It cuts out a sidelight, of course, but that can't be helped ...' Benson and Esher eventually decided to remove all references to the affair. This reflected not only the King's wishes but also their own gentlemanly sense of propriety. Esher advised the King to burn any papers concerning Lady Flora. Benson was fascinated by the business but was seemingly happy to omit all mention of it.

Worked at Windsor – found & read an extraordinary long correspondence & memorandum from M.H. Conroy (Daughter of Sir J. Conroy), for the Queen, with the hope of reinstating the family in favour. Sir J.C. was a really mischievous, unscrupulous, intriguing man. He established such an ascendancy over the Dss of Kent that he was thought to be her lover. He embezzled her money, and he hoped that when the Queen came to the Throne, he would rise too & be all-powerful. He re-invented the idea of the Duke of Cumberland wishing to poison the Queen in order to increase the idea of his own fidelity.

The Queen had a perfect horror of him; as soon as she came to the Throne she gave him a baronetcy and a pension of £3000 a year – & refused ever to see him. The horror of him appears (tho' this is very mysterious) to date from a time when the Duke of Cumberland with characteristic brutality said before her, when she was just a girl, that Conroy was her mother's lover.

This memorandum was placed in the Queen's hand. She read it with great disgust & made the frankest comments in pencil all through, 'Certainly untrue', 'never', 'a shameful lie', 'we had good reason to think he stole mother's money', and so forth. It is one of the most curious papers I have seen. The document itself is a clever one trying to make out C. to have been an old, faithful, pathetic and slighted servant whose only reward was the consciousness of his good service.

Subsequent research by Dormer Creston and Katherine Hudson has borne out these details – but this was no thanks to Benson and Esher, who did not include it in their book. In the published correspondence, Conroy is mentioned only once, in a letter from Victoria to Lord Melbourne. In a footnote, the editors explain vaguely that Conroy had made certain claims on the Queen that 'it was not considered expedient to grant', but that he did receive a baronetcy and a pension.

By these exclusions, the editors hid Victoria's knowledge of sex and her decisive dealings with Conroy. They masked her difficult and fraught adolescence and gave the impression that in the first years of her reign, and in her relationship with Melbourne, she was a spoilt, attention-seeking child who had come through young adulthood unscathed.

Benson and Esher both greatly admired Lord Melbourne. In 1904 Benson wrote to Esher, 'I am so glad that you like Lord M. I adore him – the delicious mixture of the man of the world, the chivalrous man of sentiment, the wit, the soft-hearted cynic appeals to me extraordinarily.' In the first volume, they included excerpts from thirty-five letters from Victoria to Melbourne – and 139 of Melbourne's letters to the Queen. There is no reason to suppose that this reflected an attempt to represent the original materials proportionally. In most of the published letters, Melbourne acknowledged the receipt of a letter (or several) from Victoria. Rather, the imbalance in the selection reflects the delight Benson and Esher shared in his letters. They even included excerpts from letters written by other men praising Lord Melbourne. For example, they quoted King Leopold enthusing to Victoria:

> Lord Melbourne ... is so feeling and kind-hearted that he, much more than most men who have lived so much in the *grand monde,* has preserved a certain warmth and freshness of feeling ...

Their adulation of Lord Melbourne and their desire to keep his and the Queen's reputations unsullied led the editors to err on the side of caution and exclude the Flora Hastings affair altogether. As Elizabeth Longford pointed out, it is questionable whether such silence has in fact enhanced the Queen's reputation, for it gave the impression that she was unmoved by Lady Flora's death, when 'in reality she was tortured by the affair ... for many months'. Omitting the story also meant forfeiting some fascinating material. When Lytton Strachey published his biography of Victoria in 1921 he created great drama from the Hastings incident. He used the Greville diaries as his source, drawing on both the published and unpublished entries. Although Benson and Esher had also hoped to provide drama, they lost a great deal of it by excluding these events.

Perhaps Esher remembered a letter from his old Eton tutor William Cory (Johnson), who in 1875 had written:

> Great politicians must be judged with much latitude. It is quite certain that Melbourne is one of the few public men who have not had justice done to them. The Queen can, no doubt, help greatly towards making his claims known; ... But it must be remembered that the ghost of Lady Flora haunts that part of her memory.

In deciding how to deal with Lady Flora's ghost, Benson and Esher were worried about more than the image of the young Queen. At stake was the reputation of their great favourite, Lord Melbourne. For Esher, ever cautious, the safest course was concealment.

Chapter 7

KING LEOPOLD:
THE FOREIGN ADVISER

ON THE NURSERY LANDING at Osborne House on the Isle of Wight hangs a collection of portraits of the Coburg uncles and aunts of Queen Victoria and Prince Albert. In contrast to the massive, door-sized portraits of her father's family still on view in the Waterloo Room at Windsor Castle, these are smaller and more domestic in character, hung at child's eye-level. They fit the space perfectly and are displayed in matching frames. One might assume they were painted specifically for the spot, which was Victoria and Albert's first family home. There is no equivalent display of Victoria's paternal ancestors, the Hanovers, in Osborne House. It was important to Victoria, as a young mother, that her children know their Coburg relatives and respect the heritage of their father. Victoria wrote to her Uncle Leopold following the birth of her first son: 'I <u>hope</u> and <u>pray</u> he may be like his dearest Papa. He is to be called Albert and Edward is to be his second name.' He must not be like her 'wicked' Hanoverian uncles.

King Leopold I of Belgium was the strongest influence on both Victoria and Albert for the whole of their lives. He was the younger brother of Victoria's mother and Albert's father (the Duchess of Kent and the Duke of Saxe-Coburg), both of whom encouraged and even depended upon Leopold's influence on their children.

The youngest child of his generation, Leopold was a champion of the family's influence, reputation and wealth. Using the skills imparted to him by his mother, he negotiated many of the marriages of his nephews and nieces into the major royal houses of Europe and beyond. He maintained a home in England and extensive British contacts. He corresponded with many foreign ministers. Belgium was ideally suited for stopovers and Leopold encouraged visitors. Even within the French royal family of his wife, Leopold saw himself as a leader, describing himself, curiously, as *ce qu'on appelle la loi et les prophètes* [One who calls himself the law and the prophets]. He saw himself as the peacemaker of Europe, something after Metternich, and maintained a huge correspondence in order to keep up with dynastic gossip and political events. Much of this information he passed on to Victoria and Albert.

In order to temper any perception of excessive Germanic or 'foreign' influences upon the Queen, Benson and Esher wrote in their introductory chapter that the Queen 'instinctively formed an independent judgment on any questions that concerned her … [Her advisers'] opinions were in no case allowed to do more than modify her own penetrating and clear-sighted judgment'. They emphasised this point throughout the book. The picture that emerges from the letters themselves, however, is not so clear-cut. Time and again it is evident that Leopold, Albert, Lord Melbourne and various ministers sought to influence her decisions and direct her responses.

The correspondence between Leopold and Victoria was among the first that Benson read. He immediately recognised its richness and suggested that it could have been published on its own. Leopold and Victoria corresponded weekly, using both official and private messengers. They alerted each other when they were able to use private letter carriers, as this enabled them to write more candidly, and they often requested replies by the return of the same messenger. Other letters went through the Foreign Office mail systems of their respective countries, and privacy was not assured. They wrote even more frequently after Victoria became Queen.

Although the published letters give a very strong sense of Leopold's influence, less than one tenth of the available correspondence was published, and the full character of their relationship was obscured. Throughout Victoria's childhood, as it became more likely that she would become Queen, Leopold tutored her in the arts of sovereignty. He preceded Lord Melbourne in this role. During the first year of her reign, he advised her on the procedure to be followed immediately after the death of the King, and sent his old adviser and mentor, Baron Stockmar, to be on hand to guide her. He exhorted her to heed all of Lord Melbourne's advice, which she dutifully did. He also facilitated close contacts between Victoria and her Coburg relations.

One of these was Ferdinand, a cousin of Victoria and Albert who had married the Portuguese queen, Dona Maria da Gloria II, in 1836. All four of these young people were students of Leopold's 'school' of constitutional monarchy, and they corresponded with one another frequently. To Dona Maria, Leopold wrote:

It will do well, my dear Niece, to permit me from time to time to offer You services for which my sufficiently long experience in political affairs qualifies me perhaps more than anyone else.

Your Government will have a very difficult task, the unfortunate position of Spain complicates it moreover in a rather annoying way. The first and most urgent need [Your] State has is a <u>capable ministry</u> which can gain not only the confidence of Portugal but also [that of] the rest of Europe; public prestige rests on this confidence. The finances of the kingdom require quite particular care to be taken by the Government, the welfare of the monarchy may depend on it at some time. If the army and public service are not paid regularly, it will be difficult to count on their loyalty, and this loyalty is put in doubt, especially the army, the whole/overall security of the government ceases, and from one moment to the next may be overthrown.

Leopold, who prided himself on his scientific and pragmatic understanding of government (and of matters of the heart), also wrote a three-part treatise for Ferdinand on constitutional monarchy. On his way to marry Dona Maria in Lisbon, Ferdinand had stopovers in both Brussels and London. The then sixteen-year-old Victoria mentioned in her journal that Ferdinand had brought her a copy of a document that Uncle Leopold had prepared especially for him. Victoria referred to several sections of this treatise; one was 'divided in headings of all the departments of Government', while another was titled 'Observations Générales'. The document, a fragment of which I found in Lisbon, is filled with frank advice. For example:

In days of old there existed a quite strict formality in Lisbon resembling to a great extent that of the Spanish Court. Modern customs have brought about some modifications in it but I believe that where a well established etiquette conforms to the country's habits and customs, it is indispensable. It can become a means for the government of a country where, according to ancient traditions, one fiercely holds on to status and court favours. A rank quite clearly defined has the happy result of avoiding confusion of position in society which more or less dissatisfies everybody. In England where everybody's status is fixed, this never raises these disagreeable disputes which often are the cause of lively hostilities, and I advise that the same system be followed in Portugal. That can be a little tiresome and even embarrassing sometimes: but these barriers are indispensable in a country where they have always existed and where informality could well lead to a lack of respect.

During Ferdinand's visit to England, the young Princess Victoria was not thinking only about governance. She was very impressed by him and wrote long accounts in her journal of each of the days of his visit, from 17 March to 1 April 1836: 'I think Ferdinand handsomer than [his younger brother] Augustus, his eyes are so beautiful, and he has such a lively, clever expression ... when he speaks and when he smiles ...' He seemed so grown-up and knowledgable to the young Victoria, who had been starved of the company of people her own age. The correspondence between Victoria and Ferdinand began during this time but its frequency varied over the years. Benson and Esher included none of Ferdinand's letters in the published volumes, in keeping with a more general decision to limit the Coburg correspondence.

The editors wanted the young Queen to seem naive and they may have believed her to be so. The intricacies of marriage negotiations were well known to Victoria, however, and love and romance of absorbing interest. Following her accession, King Leopold kept her up-to-date about marriages that were being brokered between the various European families: between Princess Clementine of France and various suitors; between Leopold's niece, Victoire, sister of Ferdinand, and the Duke of Nemours; even between Princess Augusta of Cambridge and Albert's brother, Ernest. The letters dealing with these negotiations, however, were not included. Such knowledge would affect the dramatics of the book; it was not consistent with the image of a sheltered young girl-queen. It would also highlight the foreign influences on Victoria, when the editors preferred to focus on her relationship with Lord Melbourne.

Benson and Esher did include many letters expressing the love and affection between Victoria and Leopold: 'I was much moved with the expressions of truly felt affection which it [your last letter] contains …'; 'We were so <u>happy</u> [being] with you, and the stay was <u>so delightful</u>, but so painfully short! It was such a joy for me to be once again under the roof of one who has ever been a father to me! I was very sad when you left us …'; 'I have ever had the care and affection of a real father for you.' Leopold frequently reminded Victoria that he had come to her mother's aid when her father died suddenly in 1820. In 1853, when Victoria named her fourth son Leopold, she wrote touchingly to her uncle:

It is a mark of love and affection which I hope you will not disapprove. It is the name which is dearest to me after Albert, and one which recalls the almost only happy days of my sad childhood; to hear 'Prince Leopold' again, will make me think of all those days.

Leopold may well have wondered why he had to wait so long to be so honoured.

Benson and Esher subtly used Victoria's correspondence with Leopold to illustrate that she was capable of warding off his influence. His advice to her sometimes bordered on the intrusive. For example, on 2 June 1838, Leopold complained that England had not supported Belgium in its recent struggle against Holland. Benson and Esher followed this with Victoria's reply, in which she quoted the opinions of Lord Melbourne and Foreign Secretary Lord Palmerston, setting out the reasons why England could not support Leopold. She softened the refusal by assuring him that England was always going to be a strong supporter of Belgian independence. But in this case, she explained, he should be using his influence to reconcile his people to the treaty with Holland, not to seek its constant revision.

The editors sought to show that Victoria embodied the British political position of the 1840s and 1850s – its strength, its fairness and its honour – in a way that would appeal to their 1907 readers. Although the letter was full of affirmations of Victoria's affection for Leopold, the Queen asserted her right and responsibility to put British interests first. Their discussion of the issue continued into the following year, with Leopold quipping that he was pleased to have 'extracted some spark of politics from your dear Majesty'. Victoria curtly advised him not to persist, as her 'political sparks ... might finally take fire ... as this is one subject on which they cannot agree'. To emphasise the importance of the exchange, Benson and Esher also included a letter from

Leopold written several years later, in which he reminded Victoria about their 'row' in 1838.

By omitting Leopold's early letters and highlighting Victoria's firmness over this issue, Benson and Esher downplayed the influence of this foreign king. In 1907, the true extent of Leopold's involvement, and his role in her political education, was deemed too potentially sensitive for publication. The same did not hold true when it came to the other foreign man in Victoria's life – Albert of Saxe-Coburg, her husband and Prince Consort.

Chapter 8

THE WELCOME FOREIGNER: PRINCE ALBERT

TIME AND AGAIN, IT has been observed by biographers how unlike his father Albert was. Born in 1819, Albert was the second son of his unhappily married parents, Ernest (Duke of Saxe-Coburg-Saalfeld) and Louise. He was, as his biographer Hector Bolitho put it, 'a stranger within a family where his father was repulsively dissolute, his mother sadly unfaithful and banished, and his brother destined to be heir to all their follies'. In many ways Albert was more like his Uncle Leopold.

The possibility that Albert was not the son of Duke Ernest was not mentioned by Benson and Esher, but David Duff has made a persuasive argument that Albert was conceived during Leopold's sad visit to Coburg in December 1818. Leopold's first wife, Charlotte, Princess of Wales, had died following the stillbirth of her first child, a son, in November 1817. Leopold was devastated. By Christmas the following year, Leopold was in Coburg visiting the already unhappy *menage* of Ernest, Louise and their firstborn son: it hurt him 'almost beyond endurance'. Louise wrote home about Leopold, describing his kindliness to her and his handsome appearance. Cognisant of both his sadness and his sensibilities, she wrote, 'He still feels with fervour what it means to be happy and loved.' Albert was born in August 1819, nine months after Leopold's visit. Theodore Martin, in his official biography of Prince Albert, quoted Duchess Louise on the special connection she perceived between Albert and Leopold on Leopold's subsequent visits: 'Albert adores his Uncle Leopold, and doesn't leave him for a moment, he looks at him lovingly, kisses him all the time and is only happy when he is near him.' 'The attraction was reciprocal, and deepened with advancing years,' observed Martin.

The Duke and Duchess divorced when Albert was five years old and the Duke remarried, to his much younger niece. This marriage 'soon broke under the shadows of spite and infidelity. Nor did the stepmother bring any strength or happiness to the young princes …' according to Hector Bolitho. The only women with whom Albert had any significant contact were his paternal grandmother, the Dowager Duchess of Coburg, who died in 1831, and his maternal step-grandmother. From the age of four Albert saw his father only occasionally. He came to depend on his brother, Ernest, and on three male mentors: his tutor, Herr Florschütz; King Leopold; and Leopold's adviser, Baron Stockmar. Florschütz continued to tutor Albert during his studies at Bonn University. Both Florschütz and Stockmar accompanied Albert on his travels to Brussels and Italy, and Stockmar joined him on his visit to England to meet Princess Victoria and, later, to marry her.

At the time of his marriage to Victoria, Albert's foreignness had roused some suspicions, but Benson and Esher revealed no such qualms. In selecting and editing correspondence relating to the marriage and to Albert's increasing influence, they created a relatively conventional narrative, in which the husband naturally asserted himself as head of his household. What they missed was the complexity of this transformation, and the extent to which both Victoria and Albert struggled to reconcile the roles of sovereign and spouse.

The 'natural' state of conjugal life, 'be one Queen or not', was that the husband must be head of the family. Hence an unresolvable dilemma – how could a young man of foreign birth, without rank or wealth, achieve his rightful place as husband when he was always to be a subject of his wife, the Queen? Victoria and Albert's cousin Ferdinand, married to the Queen of Portugal, faced the same question, as Victoria wrote to Ferdinand in 1847: 'Our positions, yours and Albert's, and Maria's and mine, are so similar, that we understand each other thoroughly.' Ferdinand's title of King, conferred upon him upon the birth of a male heir, overcame some of these problems. The title 'Prince Consort' was only conferred upon Albert seventeen years after his marriage, a delay which rankled both Victoria and Albert.

Although Victoria was Queen, she took her marriage vows to Albert very seriously, insisting that the word 'obey' be retained. This raised many questions, including political ones: as a wife, she was subject to her husband's control – but Albert was legally her subject. Lord Palmerston recognised the dilemma of the young couple. He wrote to Lord Melbourne about it: 'It seems impossible that [in this case] the husband can have over his wife those common and ordinary rights of authority.'

In the domestic sphere, Victoria attempted to establish Albert unequivocally as the head of the household, and Albert and his family expected this. In the week following their marriage Albert's brother, Ernest, reported to their uncle Leopold on Albert's 'progress'. Albert had done the 'correct thing', Ernest wrote proudly, by not hesitating to speak his opinion. All orders about the household and stables were being directed through him and thus he had become 'the great channel through whom the Queen's will' was expressed. And yet the household's status, wealth and property, the defining elements of nineteenth-century masculinity, belonged to the Queen rather than to her husband.

The tensions between being womanly and being a reigning monarch had to be constantly renegotiated by Victoria herself. She wondered in January 1840: 'What was a Queen anyway, if she had to reverse the laws of nature and put her husband below herself?' Even after reigning for fifteen years, she still sought, unsuccessfully, to reconcile the role of Queen with her perception of womanliness:

> We women are not made for governing – and if we are good women, we must dislike these masculine occupations; but there are times which force one to take interest in them *mal gré bon gré* ['whether one likes it or not'] and I do, of course, intensely.

If we read 'women' as 'wives', that is: 'We wives are not made for governing – and if we are good wives, we must dislike these masculine occupations,' one aspect of her meaning becomes clearer. Although Victoria worried about this conflict, she also affirmed her strong inclination to do this unfeminine work. In response to Albert's suggestion that their honeymoon should be longer than three days, Victoria reminded him: 'You forget, my dearest Love, that I am the Sovereign and that business can stop and wait for nothing ...'

Although Benson and Esher included these letters, there is no suggestion that they perceived Victoria's dilemma. They included the letters and memoranda of Albert in order to illustrate the natural progression of a man and his wife; the husband assumed more and more of the public role, as his wife's interests and energies necessarily devolved to the maternal and domestic.

What was a consort to a Queen? In formulating a role for himself, in some respects Albert had a *tabula rasa*; there had been no recent precedent, or at least no acceptable one. Both Albert and Victoria agreed that Queen Anne's husband, that 'stupid Prince George of Denmark', could hardly serve as a model. Lord Melbourne wryly observed to Victoria that the consort of a queen was 'an anomalous animal', neatly encapsulating both the social irregularity of the position and its breeding aspect. As a man of his era, Albert would be much more than a male version of a queen consort. By 1850 he was able to explain to the Duke of Wellington (by then an elderly statesman) that to be the consort of the Queen

> requires that the husband should entirely sink his own <u>individual existence</u> into that of his wife – that he should aim at no power by himself or for himself – should shun all contention – assume no separate responsibility before the public, but make his position entirely a part of hers – to fill up every gap which, as a woman, she would naturally leave in the exercise of her regal functions – continually and anxiously to watch every part of the public business, in order to be able to advise and assist her in any moment in any of the multifarious and difficult questions brought before her, political, or social, or personal. As the natural head of her family, superintendent of her household, man-

ager of her private affairs, sole <u>confidential</u> adviser in politics and only assistant in her communications with her officers of the Government, he is, besides, the husband of the Queen, the tutor of the royal children, the private secretary of the sovereign and her permanent minister.

In Hanover and Coburg – Albert's home turf – Salic law pertained, which barred women from reigning. Albert's doubts about Victoria's ability to fulfil her duties as sovereign may have stemmed from this. He expected not only to be head of her household, but also to be a political player. From the outset, Albert aimed to exercise 'personal power unparalleled by any Consort'.

Their uncle Leopold, as usual, offered advice. Immediately before their wedding, Albert and his party had stayed in Brussels. Leopold wrote to Victoria: 'I have already had some conversation with [Albert], and mean to talk *à fond* to him tomorrow. My wish is to see you both happy and thoroughly united and of one mind.' Leopold later told Albert's secretary, George Anson, that he had urged that Albert 'ought in business as in everything to be necessary to the Queen ... a walking dictionary for reference on any point ... [and there] should be no concealment from him on any subject'. Whether Leopold or Albert recounted these ideas to the Queen at the time is not verifiable, but – considering the emotional climate in the week before their wedding – it seems unlikely. Victoria had by now begun to resent Leopold's advice as intrusive; in a letter written shortly before her marriage (one published by Benson and Esher), she complained to Albert: '[Leopold] appears to me to be nettled because I no longer ask his advice, but dear Uncle is given to believe that he must rule the roast [roost] everywhere.'

Three months after the wedding, Albert's brother Ernest reported that despite Albert's inroads in the domestic arena, he had achieved no political role for himself. As a wife, Victoria had created 'a quiet, happy but an inglorious and dull life for him' but 'as queen she moves on another level'. Albert, however, had begun to engineer changes. Some of these were documented in memoranda, excerpts of which were included by Benson and Esher. For example, in May 1840, three months after the wedding, Albert requested that his secretary, Anson, ask Lord Melbourne to speak to the Queen about allowing him more influence. In a memorandum written by Anson after discussion with Albert, Victoria was quoted as confirming that the Prince had complained that she did not confide in him on 'trivial matters and on all matters connected with the politics of the country', which Lord Melbourne advised her she should do. At the same meeting Baron Stockmar, Leopold's adviser to Albert, agreed that the 'Queen had not started upon a right principle' by excluding the Prince from her meetings with her ministers. He also warned, however, that 'there is danger in his [Albert] wishing it all at once', and advised that Victoria 'should by degrees impart everything' to Albert. Whether he meant 'to give' or 'to communicate' is perhaps less important than the qualifier – 'everything'. Needless to say, such advice would never have been given to a female consort. Conversely, it seems unthinkable that men of such experience should have seriously imagined that Victoria – who as an adolescent had withstood Conroy's attempt to impose an extended regency, and who spoke often of enjoying queenship – would so readily relinquish a position for which she believed she had been ordained by God.

Benson thought these memoranda 'interesting enough of the early married days', but showed no interest in interrogating Albert's progress. In his 1932 biography of Albert, Hector Bolitho similarly accepted these events as unremarkable: 'When a woman is in love, her desire for power becomes less and less,' he wrote. But later biographers have been struck by the baldness of Albert's aspirations. Monica Charlot in 1991 observed, 'For Albert there was no doubt that a Queen reigning in her own right was something of an anomaly.' Victoria did come to accept Albert into a joint monarchy. This eventually occurred not so much because she yielded, however, but because she was so regularly confined by her nine pregnancies and subsequent childbirths and recoveries, which gave the men – both Albert and the politicians – more opportunity to organise matters as they thought fit.

Victoria married in February and by Easter it was known she was with child. This bolstered her husband's political position, not just his masculinity. In June, an assassination attempt – the first of many – was made on her life. Following this attack, and with all parties aware of the perils of childbirth, in July 1840 an Act was passed through Parliament naming Albert regent in the event of Victoria's death before her heir's attainment of eighteen years of age. This was an important event, yet Benson and Esher did not include any reference to it: to do so would have required mentioning a pregnancy, something they could not do. At the time, Albert wrote ecstatically to his brother:

> I am to be Regent – alone – Regent without a council. You will understand the importance of this matter and that it gives my position here in the country a fresh significance.

Albert was not yet twenty-one years old. Legally he was not yet an adult. He had been naturalised as British before his marriage, but he did not own property, yet Stockmar, Lord Melbourne, Sir Robert Peel, the Duke of Wellington and Albert's secretary, George Anson all worked behind the scenes to steer the bill through Parliament. Melbourne was delegated to raise the matter with Victoria – a delicate issue which she recorded *verbatim* in her journal thus:

> [Lord Melbourne said,] 'There is a subject I must mention, which is of great importance, & one of great emergency; perhaps you may anticipate what I mean;' (which I answered I did not), 'it is about having a Bill for a Regency' ...

A Queen consort, especially of Albert's age, would not have been accorded the same responsibilities. Victoria's mother had been declared Regent in 1820 when Victoria was heir presumptive – but she was a mature woman who had acted as regent for her son in Leiningen for several years during her first widowhood. In Albert's case, this regency was for the heir apparent. As Monica Charlot observed, 'The spirit of the age certainly was on Albert's side.' Albert acknowledged this himself just before the birth of their first child, the Princess Royal, when he wrote to his brother:

> I wish you could see us here and see in us a couple united in love and unanimity. Now Victoria is also ready to give up something for my sake, I everything for her sake ... Do not think I lead a submissive life. On the contrary, here, where the lawful position of the man is so, I have formed a prize life for myself.

During Victoria's confinement for the six weeks following the birth, Albert conducted Privy Council meetings, wrote correspondence on her behalf and met with her ministers. Again, Benson and Esher included no reference to this in their selections, although Victoria noted it in her journal and Albert related it to his brother.

Albert's progress over the next year was steady. By May, Victoria was again pregnant. Many of the letters and memoranda bearing her name from these years were drafted by Albert, and the editors had to establish a protocol for presenting these. Benson wrote to Esher:

> A point of considerable difficulty has turned up ... there are a good many memoranda signed <u>Victoria R.</u> These are sometimes in the first person singular 'I' and sometimes in the first person plural 'we'.
>
> But when they are in the first person singular, the word 'I' always stands for Prince Albert.
>
> This will cause great confusion.

Victoria's use of the third person singular – 'she' – throughout her letters was retained. She may have used 'we' more frequently in verbal exchanges, but in memoranda written by Albert, 'we' referred to the royal couple. A footnote was occasionally given explaining authorship, but frequently this was inconsistent, suggesting that the editors were sometimes unsure.

In 1839, before her marriage, the first great constitutional problem of Victoria's reign arose: her reluctance to part with Lord Melbourne as Prime Minister. Following a debate in the House of Commons, Melbourne resigned. When the elderly Duke of Wellington refused the Queen's offer to form a new Tory government, she had to turn to Sir Robert Peel, the Conservative leader in the House of Commons. According to custom, a change of government was accompanied by a change of the personnel of the monarch's household; convention held that the new Prime Minister should nominate the Ladies of the Bedchamber. The existing Ladies had been chosen on Lord Melbourne's advice and were thus predominantly Whigs, with no Conservative connections or sympathies. Peel demanded that this custom be observed. Victoria refused.

Benson and Esher documented this crisis more thoroughly than they did most other topics. They showed Peel to have had none of Melbourne's ability to persuade the young Queen, who had no intention of giving in. There is room for debate as to her motives. Was she trying to hold to a political principle? Did she feel a particular attachment to her ladies? She had only been Queen for a little over twelve months and perhaps felt some insecurity in the running of her Court. Or did she realise that she might be able to return Lord Melbourne's ministry to power? The documents in the *Letters*, especially her journal entries, tend to suggest the latter. Writing in her diary midway through the crisis, she recorded: 'Lord Melbourne said we might be beat. I said I never would yield.' The following days produced a torrent of letters and memoranda, which Benson and Esher selected and edited to great dramatic effect.

Peel finally refused to take office, being unable to secure a majority. Melbourne continued as Prime Minister. When he resigned again in 1841, Victoria was in the early part of her second pregnancy, which had followed uncomfortably closely after the first; her first two babies were born a mere fifty weeks apart. What Benson and Esher's selection does not reveal is that Albert and Melbourne, without Victoria's knowledge, discussed how to avert a second Bedchamber Crisis and sent Anson to meet with Sir Robert Peel to 'prepare the ground' for a change of government. Following these meetings, Victoria signed a memorandum instructing the Prime Minister to appoint only those members of her household who would be sitting in Parliament. She retained the right to appoint her own Ladies of the Bedchamber, although the Prime Minister could object to particular individuals 'in case he would deem their appointment injurious to the Government'. There were still some upsetting scenes in the Court, which suggests that Victoria was not happy with the situation. This in turn suggests that the memorandum was drafted by Albert.

Benson and Esher included many letters from this period, mostly between Victoria and Melbourne. In the end only three of Victoria's ladies were asked to resign. Melbourne declared that his time in Victoria's service was 'the proudest as well as the happiest part of his life'. Sir Robert Peel and his Cabinet were finally sworn into office in September 1841, and Albert was made chairman of the Arts Commission for the rebuilding of Parliament. In contrast to Victoria, Albert liked Peel and forged a strong working relationship and friendship with the new Prime Minister. The Whig sympathies of the Court were shifting. In any case, Peel had won by a substantial majority in the general election and could not easily have been undermined, even by the monarch.

By August 1841, Albert believed that the 'Court from highest to lowest' had been brought 'to a proper sense of the position of the Queen's husband'. Senior statesmen like Melbourne and Palmerston were non-plussed by Albert's fervour, but also admiring of his tenacity. Monica Charlot observed that the two Whig statesmen were 'caricatures of English aristocrats' – gregarious, displaying an air of indolence, epicures, accomplished in the art of witty exchanges after dinner and fond of the company of women – whereas Albert was the opposite – 'Germanic, solitary, intolerant, finding social life time-wasting, and women of little interest'. Albert was thirty years their junior, with values and ideas of which they were sceptical. Despite these differences, they admired his good qualities, although Albert remained highly critical of them.

It seems that these politicians saw no reason to question the ambitions of a male consort to a sovereign; it was only natural that Albert should seek to exercise more power. The response had been very different when Queen Adelaide, consort of Victoria's uncle, King William IV, was thought to have influenced the King during the reform agitation. On one occasion, her carriage was assailed by an angry mob. When the government resigned in 1834, *The Times* declared, 'The Queen has done it all'; the headline was placarded all over London. It was not all plain sailing for Albert. In 1854 he was (falsely) accused of political meddling and declared a traitor by the broadsheets; he was even rumoured to have been sent to the Tower of London. Nevertheless, the double standard persisted into the 1900s, and Benson and Esher saw nothing unusual in Albert's desire to expand his role.

Nor did Benson and Esher seek to downplay Albert's influence, as they had done with King Leopold. Albert was more foreign than Leopold, but as the Queen's husband and, to a lesser extent, as father of the heir, his growing power was perfectly acceptable. The part Victoria's pregnancies played in his ascension got no mention. Victoria did come to acknowledge how competent Albert was and increasingly deferred to his judgment. Their marriage remained a partnership, albeit one very different from the conventional Victorian vision of marriage, and one requiring more complex negotiation than the published letters would suggest.

QUEEN VICTORIA'S CONFINEMENTS

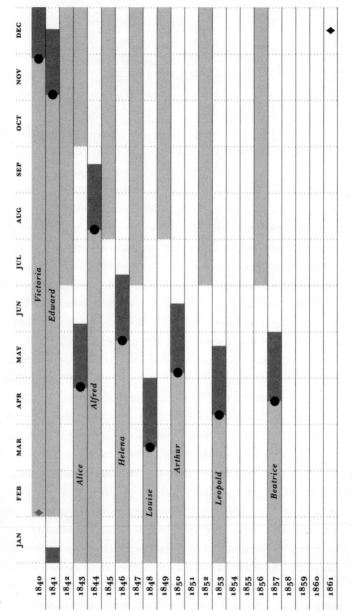

Marriage ◆   Birth ●   Pregnancy ▓   6 Week Domicilary Confinement ▓   Albert's Death ◆

Chapter 9

WOMEN'S BUSINESS

BENSON FOUND WOMEN'S LETTERS to be 'very tiresome'. Consequently very few of the thousands of letters Victoria exchanged with her female relations and friends were included. She corresponded with many women, including: her half-sister, Princess Feodore of Hohenlohe-Langenburg; her aunt Louise, Queen of the Belgians, wife of Leopold and daughter of King Louis-Philippe of France; her cousin Victoire, Duchess of Nemours and sister of Ferdinand; her sister-in-law Alexandrine, Duchess of Saxe-Coburg from 1842; and Dona Maria, Queen of Portugal.

The small number of women's letters in the published volumes cannot be attributed to the editors' ignorance of their existence. As early as March 1904, Benson described a set of letters from Princess Feodore as 'simple family letters, full of detail, such as the Queen loved. But the writing is troublesome ... They would be interesting enough just to skim through if they were printed.' Feodore's handwriting is far easier to decipher than Lord Melbourne's, and Benson was more than willing to struggle with Melbourne's hiero-glyphics. Excerpts from four of Feodore's letters were pub-lished, but there survive hundreds more, written weekly over a forty-four year period, in the Royal Archives at Windsor and at the Hohenlohe-Zentral Archive in Germany. Surely such a long friendship would have revealed a unique side of Victoria's nature, especially given the intimacies of sisterhood and the particular circumstances of these two women? Feodore was married to an elderly, impoverished duke and struggled to raise her children in loneliness and isolation in Germany, far away from her mother, who remained in England, while Victoria became Queen, married and had a large number of children.

Another entry in Benson's diary confirms that women's letters were available: 'finished the last vol. of documents – the letters of Q. Louise [of the Belgians] up to the end of 1841 …' Esher and Knollys discussed the whereabouts of Victoria's correspondence with Alexandrine in 1905. Esher also knew about the letters from Feodore and Queen Adelaide to Victoria's official governess, the Duchess of Northumberland, concerning Victoria's welfare under the Kensington System. These were drawn to the editors' attention very late in the editing. Even if they had been found earlier, however, it is unlikely that they would have been included, given their subject matter.

The Queen of Portugal's monthly letters to Victoria, written in a very idiosyncratic French with little or no punctuation, are held in the Royal Archives, Windsor. Benson and Esher included one letter from Maria, congratulating Victoria on her engagement, but Maria wrote many more over the following thirteen years. Only six of Victoria's replies have been found to date in Lisbon and discovering more is unlikely – as Maria confessed to Victoria, 'I have the rather bad habit of tearing up letters after I have replied to them.'

Victoria and Maria met in person on only two occasions,

both times in London as children. Maria, just seven weeks older than Victoria, came to the Portuguese throne as a fifteen-year-old in politically tumultuous times. By the time she married Prince Ferdinand (Victoria's cousin), when she was seventeen, she had already been betrothed to her uncle and then married to her stepmother's brother, who died two months after their wedding. After negotiations between the various chancelleries of Europe, a marriage contract was signed in Coburg with Baron Stockmar as one of the signatories. Maria married Ferdinand first by proxy and then in person in Lisbon in 1836. Their first child was born the following year. (Bismarck was, later in the century, to characterise the House of Saxe-Coburg as the 'stud farm of Europe'.)

At the start of their correspondence, the letters between Victoria and Maria were brief, and Maria mentioned Ferdinand only rarely. This may have been in deference to Victoria's still being a single girl. After Victoria's marriage, and especially after her first child was born, their letters became much more personal and familiar. Victoria was impressed by Maria's devotion, almost fealty, to Ferdinand. In a letter to Leopold before her accession in 1837, Victoria wrote of Maria, 'One good quality, however, she has, which is her excessive fondness for, and real obedience to, Ferdinand.' After Victoria's wedding day, the more experienced Maria wrote:

> I cannot stop myself from writing you two little words of felicitation on your marriage. I assure you that I have thought of you much during the 10th. In truth a wedding day is a day quite solemn and quite disagreeable to pass. This always happens, even for anybody who loves such occasions a lot, but once this is over, one is entirely at

one's ease. I have read in the newspapers [about] the whole ceremony. It must have been quite beautiful, and I am certain that Albert has made a great impression and that he was much praised. Also I have much admired your enormous composure throughout the ceremony. I assure you that I was much more embarrassed than you. I hope that God will grant my wishes and you will be the happiest of women. I also hope that soon, too, you will give me little <u>cousins</u> whom I shall love with all my heart.

In 1905, no published letters by a woman would have included references to pregnancy or personal health, so it is not surprising to find that Benson and Esher omitted nearly all mention of these matters. Their belief that they could show the 'full development of the character of the Queen' without these topics also reflected their particularly narrow understanding of female experience. They even went so far as to record the arrival of Victoria's first child in a footnote, several pages after its chronological place. This downplaying of the birth of the Prince of Wales – the first male heir to be born to a Queen regnant for hundreds of years – probably reflected specific directions from King Edward VII concerning 'personal and private' material, particularly concerning himself.

As young queens, Victoria and Maria shared an unusual position. For them both, pregnancy, childbirth and recovery occupied much of their time during the early years of their reigns. During the twenty-one years of her marriage, Victoria gave birth to nine children, all of whom survived into adulthood. During the first five years of her marriage, Victoria was either pregnant or recovering from childbirth for all but sixteen of sixty months – that is, for nearly 75 per cent of the time (as illustrated on page 124).

These figures stated baldly hardly show the impact these pregnancies and births had on the queens' public and private lives. Particular aspects of pregnancy and childbirth, such as anxiety at the start of each new pregnancy, ailments such as nausea, bleeding, tiredness and changes in appetite, and the potential complications during and after birth, were not easily accommodated within a public life of levées, soirées, official visits and political crises. Rather dramatically, a major military challenge to Dona Maria's power coincided with the onset of her first labour in 1837 and remained unresolved for several weeks. In 1842, Victoria too experienced a collision of public and private: arriving in Edinburgh in the first week of September, she refused to take part in the customary welcoming procession through the city. The Scots were very critical. Her third child, Princess Alice, was born on 25 April 1843; calculating backwards suggests that Victoria's arrival in Edinburgh would have coincided with the symptoms of early pregnancy – probably exacerbated by the sea voyage from London – which may explain her reluctance. (She was persuaded to drive through the streets in procession several hours later to placate the waiting crowds. Perhaps the nausea had passed.)

Despite these women's privileged living conditions, rank and wealth in the nineteenth century provided no guarantee against disease and infection. The letters between these two royal mothers show their many anxieties concerning their own health and that of their children: breastfeeding and wet nurses, smallpox inoculations, weaning, teething, then education; anxiety about their husbands' health and the dangers of hunting, for example. The roles of queen, wife and mother all had their inherent dangers: these women experienced assassination attempts; epidemics of scarlet fever, cholera and typhoid; the high incidence of tuberculosis; the deaths in childbirth of female friends and relatives. In addition, they each had to carry out their duties in public, with little allowance made for their worries or discomforts. In sharing their anxieties (as well as more frivolous gossip), Maria and Victoria exchanged support and information.

There was a delicate and poignant occasion in October 1840, just weeks before Queen Victoria's first confinement. Dona Maria had recently given birth to her third child, her first daughter, who was stillborn. Ferdinand wrote to Victoria and Albert to tell them the sad news before Maria wrote to Victoria a month later. In seeking to alleviate any alarm Victoria might have felt, Maria reverted to a more light-hearted style:

My dear Victoria

Well, for quite a long time that I have not been able to have the great pleasure of writing to you but you know the reason for that quite well from all of Ferdinand's letters. I hope that my affair will not have affected you too much, for in your state it is necessary to try and avoid this if that is possible. It hardly ever happens; but I am convinced now that you will be quite safe and that you will present us with a very beautiful and very bonny, little male Cousin ...

Dona Maria was to experience the premature deaths of four babies. In all she gave birth to eleven children before she died in her thirty-fourth year following the birth of a stillborn child in 1853.

In their discussions of motherhood, the two women hid, indeed were expected to hide, their true emotions and anxieties, both negative and positive: their fears of pain, of failure, and of death, and their delight in parenthood. But they found ways to express, with humility and cheerfulness, their feelings, and this is particularly evident in Dona Maria's writing. Maria lifted the mask a little when she wrote to Victoria about the forthcoming confinement of Ferdinand's sister, Victoire, the Duchess of Nemours:

> Victoire has written me a letter which has given us very great pleasure for she announces that she will present us a nephew or niece; she desires very much a boy, may God grant her that; she or he will be born at the same time as mine which I find very agreeable for us both; I wished that that were already over for her for I find that the first is a terrible event.

Writing about a third person, Maria could express her fears more openly than when describing her own experiences. Victoria was similarly direct when she wrote to her newly pregnant eldest daughter, Vicky, in 1858. In this correspondence she frequently raged against pregnancy and childbirth:

> I think much more of our being like a cow or a dog at such moments; when our poor nature becomes so very animal and unecstatic – but for you, dear, if you are sensible and reasonable and not in ecstasy nor spending your day with nurses and wet nurses, which is the ruin of many a refined and intellectual young lady, without adding to her real maternal duties, a child will be a great resource. Above all, dear girl, do remember never to lose the modesty of a young girl towards others (without being prude); though you are married don't become a matron to whom everything can be

said and who minds saying nothing herself – I remained to a particular degree (indeed feel so now) and often feel schocked [sic] at the confidences of other married ladies. I fear abroad they are very indelicate about these things …

These letters are in direct contrast to her surviving journal entries from those early mothering years, and to her letters to her women friends. Victoria delighted in showing her baby daughter off to Lord Melbourne before Privy Council meetings and in standing over the crib as the baby 'smiled up at her and cooed'. Benson and Esher probably did not see the later letters of Victoria to her daughter; had they done so we can be sure they would not have been published.

Maria and Victoria both adhered absolutely to the idea of patriarchy, and with their husbands sought to implement it in their domestic lives. In reply to Maria's letter of 8 May 1842, Victoria wrote:

All that you tell me in your letter of 8th in reference to your position has interested me greatly, and I assure you that I share entirely your opinion, the husband should always be first; I'm doing <u>everything</u> in order that it be thus – and I am always saddened that he must be below me in rank; for it pains me to be Queen and he merely the Prince; but in my heart, and in my house, he comes first and is the master and head …

In 1847, Maria praised Ferdinand and his executive abilities to Victoria, who replied:

You have spoken to me with quite some warmth about your concern that Ferdinand be known to the world for …

his great experience and his knowledge of political matters, as well as for his strong and noble character ... In
Ferdinand you have foremost a man superior to those
around him, and a soul who will share all your sentiments;
– I can therefore only give you the good advice to continue
to ensure his place in your counsels, which is due to him
and which he will always employ with much success for
you as Queen, as Wife and as Mother.

The inclusion of Victoria's correspondence with Maria,
and with her other female confidantes, would have given a
much fuller picture of her life and personality. These young
women were grappling with similar worries and dilemmas,
both as wives and mothers and as sovereigns. Their letters
helped them to make sense of their experiences and to offset
their sense of social isolation. Benson and Esher recognised
none of these issues, preferring instead to focus almost exclu-
sively on Victoria's relationships with men. As they wrote in
their Introduction, 'Confident, in a sense, as she was, she had
the feminine instinct strongly developed of dependence upon
some manly adviser.' They selected and edited her letters
with this 'dependence' in mind. In the process, they omitted
key aspects of Victoria's character, an omission that would
persist for at least the first half of the twentieth century.

Chapter 10

THE QUEEN AND HER MINISTERS

As Lord Esher was editing the letters he was becoming ever closer to the King, but he found that the King was not as powerful as he might wish. He and the King's private secretary, Lord Knollys, believed Edward VII was not being 'kept informed' as he should have been by his ministers. It is ironical that St John Brodrick, Secretary of State for War at the beginning of Edward's reign, held that one of the greatest impediments to open ministerial consultation with the monarch was Esher's closeness to the King and his presence on two important committees, the South African War Committee and then the War Office Reconstruction Committee. In his memoirs, Brodrick recalled:

> Before long it became clear that by the time any decision had come to the point when Cabinet could lay it before the Sovereign, the issue had been largely pre-judged, on the incomplete premises of an observer who had no official status.

In other words, Esher, whether intentionally or not, had constituted himself the unofficial adviser of the Crown, and his ambition to control what he termed 'the hornet's nest' (the War Office) from the outside became for a moment the ruling passion of his life.

Queen Victoria's letters revealed to Esher a monarch who, with her consort, was fully in charge of her ministers. He saw the early years of Victoria's reign as a time when individual ministers such as Peel and Aberdeen, and even those as 'headstrong as Palmerston or as truculent as Russell', were careful not only 'to keep the Sovereign informed' but also to ask the sovereign's advice 'before final decisions were reached in Cabinet upon all questions of substance'. It was, Esher claimed, 'a system of Government which was brought almost to perfection in the middle of the last century'.

Esher was hugely admiring of Queen Victoria's and the Prince's industriousness and their executive abilities: 'Certainly the work done by her and the P. Consort was amazing … it was in their heyday of youth and prosperity.' Whatever he hoped for his King, he knew that Edward was more than sixty years old and was never going to exert himself to this extent. Nevertheless, Victoria's methods became for Esher a blueprint for the proper relationship between a sovereign and his or her ministers. In August 1905, he set out his ideas in a long letter to Lord Knollys:

I can only tell you, that after studying now, with great completeness, the history of the relation of the Crown to different Administrations, extending over sixty years, … that the monarchical system as understood by Sir Robert Peel, Lord Aberdeen, Lord Palmerston and Lord Derby, and as worked by them in conjunction with the Queen, was of

immense value to the State and to the people of this country ... the Sovereign's interferences and tenacity, both of
which were very remarkable, had on several very vital occasions stayed the action of a Minister, when such action
involved risks and perils which reflection convinced him
and his colleagues they were not justified in incurring.

There is one very notable example, which is the action
of the Sovereign in restraining Lord John Russell in 1859,
when, but for the tenacity of the Crown, England would
have been mixed up in the Austro-Italian war ...

It would only waste your time if I were to amplify
examples ... [but they] are object lessons which, if the dig-
nity of High Office under the Crown is to be maintained,
the present Prime Minister and his successor ought to
take them seriously to heart.

Esher ensured that plenty of room was found for such
examples in the published letters. This was history with a
purpose: to show present-day ministers their proper place.
The centrepiece was Victoria's insistence on the dismissal of
her Foreign Secretary, Lord Palmerston, in 1851.

When Victoria first came to the throne, Palmerston was a
man of fifty-three. He was still handsome and vigorous, and
still bore the nickname 'Cupid' from his university days. Just
prior to Victoria's marriage to Albert, Palmerston married
his paramour of thirty years, the sister of Lord Melbourne,
Emily Cowper, a widowed lady-in-waiting to Victoria. As a
pair of twenty-year-olds, Victoria and Albert were amused
by the 'elderly lovers' (who were in their fifties): 'I am sure it
will make you smile,' Victoria wrote to Albert. 'They make
up a century between them,' Albert quipped.

As Foreign Secretary in the Whig governments of the

1830s, Palmerston had become a major figure in international politics. He had secured the independence of the Belgian throne with Leopold at its head, assisted Dona Maria II in Portugal and Queen Isabella in Spain, been involved in Greece and Turkey, and resisted Russian encroachments in the Middle East. He came to be cordially detested by absolutist monarchs and their ministers, and he remained ever suspicious of French expansionist intentions, which he thwarted at every opportunity. His relations with Victoria were at first friendly, during the years of the Melbourne ministry and before her marriage. Alongside Lord Melbourne and Lady Cowper, he frequently dined with the young Queen. Palmerston advised Victoria in much the same avuncular tone and manner as did Melbourne, and Victoria welcomed this advice. Benson and Esher included a sample of his gentlemanly humour in the *Letters*:

> Viscount Palmerston ... begs to state that he has reason to believe, from what Count Pollon [Sardinian Minister to England] said to him in conversation two days ago, that the Duke of Lucca [an independent Italian state] has a notion that Sovereign Princes who have had the honour of dining with your Majesty, have been invited by note not by card. If that should be so, and if your Majesty should invite the Duke of Lucca to dine at the Palace before his departure, perhaps the invitation should be made by note instead of card, as it was when the Duke last dined at the Palace. Your Majesty may think this is a small matter, but the Duke is a small Sovereign.

After her marriage, Victoria began to express stronger views about foreign policy. The change became more obvious after May 1840, when Albert solicited Melbourne's, Anson's and Stockmar's help to persuade (or even force) Victoria to allow him access to the ministerial papers. His access to these documents gave him a surer footing from which to comment on foreign affairs. Benson and Esher included several letters that revealed this shift. In September 1840, Victoria told Leopold that 'Albert, who sends his love, is much occupied with the Eastern Affairs.' A few months later, she wrote a long and closely argued reply to Palmerston's letter of 11 November 1840 on the same topic, which sounds much more like Albert than Victoria. (Their first child was born ten days later.)

After 1841, Palmerston was out of office and had little to do with the Court. Victoria dealt with Aberdeen as Foreign Secretary, who was more malleable. But upon Palmerston's return as Foreign Secretary in 1846 in Lord John Russell's Whig government, relations grew increasingly hostile. The Queen and Prince Albert frequently complained about not being informed in advance of Palmerston's decisions. Following the congenial relationship between Victoria and Palmerston in the early years of her reign, Albert's influence in these subsequent years was striking. He had persuaded Victoria that Palmerston's urbanity was rakish.

Although many of these letters were published, they were so numerous that Benson could make only a representative selection. Very few of them carry Albert's name, although from 1843 he wrote summaries of every interview the Queen held, penned memoranda and even gradually began to draft many of her official letters.

In August 1850, Victoria wrote to John Russell and directed him to pass a message on to Palmerston:

> With reference to the conversation about Lord Palmerston which the Queen had with Lord John Russell the other

day, and Lord Palmerston's disavowal that he ever intended any disrespect to her by the various neglects of which she has had so long and so often to complain, she thinks it right, in order <u>to prevent any mistakes in the future</u>, shortly to explain <u>what she expects of her Foreign Secretary.</u> She requires:

(1) That he will distinctly state what he proposes in a given case, in order that the Queen may know as distinctly to <u>what</u> she has given her Royal sanction;

(2) Having <u>once given</u> her sanction to a measure, that it may not be arbitrarily altered or modified by the Minister; such an act she must consider as failing in sincerity towards the Crown, and justly to be visited by the exercise of her Constitutional right of dismissing that Minister. She expects to be kept informed of what passes between him and the Foreign Ministers before important decisions are taken based on that intercourse; to receive Foreign Despatches in good time, and to have the drafts for approval sent to her in sufficient time to make herself acquainted with their contents before they must be sent off. The Queen thinks it best that Lord John Russell should show this letter to Lord Palmerston.

Six months later, in March 1851, the Queen again reminded Lord Russell that he too 'must keep her constantly informed of what is going on, and of the temper of the parties in and out of the Parliament'.

Russell was in a difficult position. He was not confident of the Queen's good opinion of him and did not want to displease her. He did not entirely approve of Palmerston's conduct – but he could not afford to offend the Radical and Liberal MPs who admired Palmerston, and on whose support his government relied. Throughout 1851, Victoria was irritated by Palmerston's continued attempts to assert his judgments on matters which she believed could put her in conflict with her government. For example, in October, there ensued weeks of correspondence between the Queen, Russell and Palmerston on the visit of the Hungarian patriot Lajos Kossuth, one of the severest critics of Austria and Russia. Only three years earlier, Kossuth had sought but ultimately failed to overthrow the Austrian monarchy by force. Victoria and Albert looked upon the young Emperor Franz Josef of Austria as a respected fellow monarch, but Palmerston had used England's influence to protect Kossuth when he fled to Turkey and now wanted to meet him. Palmerston hoped to evade official censure by entertaining Kossuth in his own home, as a private citizen. For Palmerston to host Kossuth (either officially or privately) in 1851 might be compared to a Foreign Secretary of today entertaining a Chinese pro-democracy activist. Victoria declared that if Palmerston did so, she would sack him; he backed down. Within ten days, however, Palmerston had resumed his antagonistic attitude, receiving a Radical deputation from London who congratulated him on his support of Kossuth and denounced Tsar Nicholas and the Emperor Franz Josef. Greville, the Secretary to the Privy Council at the time, thought this the worst thing Palmerston had ever done.

There was another clash with Palmerston late in 1851. On 2 December, the anniversary of the battle of Austerlitz and of the coronation of Napoleon I, Louis Napoleon dissolved the National Assembly in Paris and arrested its leaders. By these actions he staged a *coup d'état*, effectively making himself president for life (he declared himself Emperor Napoleon III in 1852). The English Ambassador,

Lord Normanby, was ordered to remain neutral, but Palmerston congratulated the French Ambassador in London, Count Walewski, telling him he approved of the *coup*. When Normanby told the French Foreign Minister in Paris that England was remaining neutral, he was hugely embarrassed to be told that Palmerston had already offered his warm support.

In the published letters about this affair, there are two from Lord Normanby's wife. The first is to Lord Normanby's brother, who was an equerry to Prince Albert. She described the difficult and dangerous situation her husband found himself in and asked about the general feeling in England. The second letter was to Victoria, and this is how the Queen found out about Palmerston's 'double-crossing' of Normanby. She insisted that Palmerston resign. In Parliament, Russell ill-advisedly read out the letter in which Victoria set out what she expected of her Foreign Secretary (quoted above), in order to exonerate himself in his minister's demise. Palmerston never forgave him.

The difficulty Benson faced in dealing with these letters was that the new King showed no sign of wanting to adopt his parents' assertive style. Unlike his mother, King Edward VII welcomed the growth of democracy that had led to the reduction of the monarch's power. He supported the *Third Reform Act* of 1884, which amongst other things gave the vote to agricultural labourers, and had even contrived to watch a reform march in London from the balcony of the home of a friend, Lord Carrington. Upon seeing him, the crowd had halted and sung 'God Bless the Prince of Wales'. The Queen, however, was not enthusiastic about the *Third Reform Act*, which she believed would be destabilising. She was anxious 'to avert serious dangers so much desired by

Radicals and Republicans'. Hence the editors' dilemma: they could not glorify Victoria's assertive approach to her ministers *too* much, for fear of being seen to suggest that the present King's handling of his ministers was inferior.

Moreover, King Edward VII was fond of Lord Palmerston, who had been a mentor to him when his parents despaired of him. Palmerston was one of several ministers who pleaded unsuccessfully with the Queen to allow the Prince to learn from her about the monarch's role or to be given some useful work. In the end, Esher softened the image of the assertive Queen and her clashes with her Foreign Secretary. Many passages of criticism of Palmerston were removed. Victoria and Albert's disparaging nickname for him, 'Pilgerstein', was dropped. (The nickname was derived from a German version of his name, *Pilger*, which was German for a palmer, a pilgrim who returned from the Holy Land with a palm frond. As Victoria's biographer Elizabeth Longford wrote, 'No doubt they got a sardonic kick out of visualizing Palmerston, the devil's son, disguised as a holy man with staff and scrip … inflaming foreign nationalists, establishing constitutional governments, picking quarrels with despots.')

In the end, Esher's caution again won out over Benson's sense of drama. The initial selection included Victoria's 1850 comment to King Leopold that 'The House of Commons are becoming very unmanageable & troublesome, and try to take the powers entirely into their own hands.' Before showing the pages to the King, however, Esher insisted that the last phrase be deleted. Benson unsuccessfully protested, arguing that it was of 'great historical value – 60 years on!' But present considerations were determining the documentation of the past. Although Esher hoped that Edward might come to control his ministers as Victoria had done, he finally had to dilute the anti-democratic instincts of the mother so as not to offend the son.

Chapter 11

THE KING'S CENSORS

FROM THE START OF the project, Benson and Esher had been aware that the King must approve their work. As the time came to seek his formal approval, the editors, particularly Esher, became very nervous. Although Esher was by now an intimate friend of the King, nothing could be taken for granted. Esher had confided to Benson that the King was sometimes a 'touchy person'. If Esher were to incur the King's disapproval, it would exact an enormous price – personally, socially and financially. Consequently, before he gave the proofs to the King, he read them once more. Previously, he had been reading with an eye to fashioning a readable and dramatic portrait of the Queen. This time, he needed to see things through the King's sensitive eyes. Conscious that these two perspectives were not always aligned, he contrived various plans to avoid any possibility of a showdown with the King.

In November 1905, Esher advised John Murray and Arthur Benson that the King's approval for Volume I would take about a week. They therefore expected to hear from Esher at least before Christmas. Murray in particular was impatient for news; the first two volumes, almost 1200 pages, were now typeset and sitting in his printery in Scotland. Once Volume I was given the 'all clear' for printing, he could have a 'stereotype' created, break up the metal type and have more trays and letters available for the third volume. (He had already purchased more type for the project and was unwilling to incur any further expense.) Although changes to the typeset text were time-consuming and expensive, this was the last opportunity for alterations.

By Christmas, there was no news. Both Murray and Benson now wrote constantly to Esher – about the plates, the preface, the prospectus, the translation of French and German passages, about Volumes II and III – for almost any reason, in order to speed Volume I to publication.

Why did Esher take so long to achieve what he had predicted would take a week? In the last months of 1905 and the early months of 1906, he was busily involved in the War Office Territorial Committee and in the establishment and chairing of the Army Review Committee – but this also meant that he was in frequent, often daily, contact with the King.

John Murray was hugely frustrated by the delays. Both he and Benson diplomatically urged Esher along, reiterating time and again the problems of the type being 'tied up' and their inability to proceed with the editing of Volume III until it could be set. They always employed a gentlemanly and deferential turn of phrase: 'This is not to hurry you in any way, but only to explain exactly how we are situated,' Benson wrote to Esher in June 1906.

In August 1906, the King left England to visit Germany and Austria. Murray and Benson continued to wait for royal approval, while Esher and Knollys adjourned to their respective retreats in the Scottish Highlands. Benson was becoming hot and bothered. After receiving yet another impatient letter from Murray, he shot back a reply marked 'Private':

> As to the Queen's letters, I can <u>well</u> understand your feeling ... I will tell you frankly and confidentially that I am meditating a final coup – withdrawing from the Editorship. If much objection is taken to what we have done, and if much rearrangement &c becomes necessary, I think I shall say plainly that I will have nothing more to do with it. Of course it would mean throwing away some money &c but it will give you some idea of how these delays irritate one. Royalties have no conception how much trouble they give and no one ever tells them. It is not want of consideration so much as the deplorable kind of education they receive.
>
> I have mentioned this as yet to no one but yourself; but if I can't get things to move, I shall write to Esher in the same sense shortly. Please regard this as wholly confidential.
>
> Ever yours,
>
> ACB

Benson in this instance was being disingenuous. Like Esher, he could play games when it suited, and he was merely trying to placate Murray. In his diary entry for the same day he wrote: 'Irritable letter from Murray ... but I took the wind out of his sails by telling him quite frankly that I was thinking of giving up the editorship myself!' But Benson, ever conscious of his financial position, never seriously intended to carry out his threat.

Esher, meanwhile, knowing that the King would not read all the letters himself, chose two men whom the King would respect to check the revised proofs. The first was Arthur Bigge, Lord Stamfordham, Queen Victoria's last private secretary and later Keeper of the Privy Purse. An interested and conservative critic, he was chosen because of his long and close association with Victoria and his current position in the Royal Household. The second was John Morley, a Gladstonian Liberal, a member of Parliament and of Cabinet and a successful author. Benson was not consulted about this process and remained unaware of it.

Bigge wrote to Esher saying that he disagreed with the publishing of *any* of the late Queen's letters or journals, and implied that Esher had agreed with him: 'I am glad that you and I agree in deprecating in the publishing of any letters and journals: however the King, I suppose, has well considered this particular case.' Bigge mistakenly believed that the pages he was reviewing had already been approved by the King – a misunderstanding orchestrated by Esher. The King had seen some of the Queen's early letters 'referring to family matters', but certainly not the whole volume. Consequently, Bigge excused himself from suggesting significant cuts, lest he seem presumptuous in questioning the King's judgment. He did, however, question the inclusion of some of the letters between Lord Melbourne and Queen Victoria before her marriage: 'There is a good deal in there which I cannot help thinking was never intended for publication; which is of no importance historically and would only supply matter for gossip and possibly ill-natured criticism.' In outlining his concerns, he revealed a true courtier's mindset: protective of the image of the Queen and of her memory; submissive towards the present King; anxious that material deemed 'private' not be disseminated into the public domain. He sent a detailed list of objections to Lord Knollys:

In the extract from the Queen's Journal describing the events of the CORONATION p. 153 there are passages especially referring to Lord Melbourne and to the Queen's conversation after the ceremony which strike me as unsuitable for publication.

The extract to which he referred was eventually printed in its entirety and included such passages as:

My excellent Lord Melbourne, who stood very close to me throughout the whole ceremony, was completely over-come ... when [he] knelt down and kissed my hand, he pressed my hand, and I grasped his with all my heart, at which he looked up with his eyes filled with tears and seemed much touched ...

Victoria went on to record affectionate comments made by Melbourne after the ceremony: 'He asked kindly if I was tired; and said the Sword he carried (the first Sword of State) was excessively heavy. I said that the Crown hurt me a good deal. He was very much amused ...' He congratulated Victoria 'again and again' throughout the evening. At one point, 'with tears in his eyes ... he said, "You did it so well – excellent! ... It's a thing that you can't give a person advice upon; it must be left to the person."' Perhaps it was the emotional intimacy which Bigge found to be 'unsuitable', as he also objected to:

letters to Lord Lansdowne pp. 222 & 225 in which the Queen is 'sadly disappointed' at Lord M's not coming to dine especially 'as she felt so happy at the thought of his <u>not</u> dining elsewhere and <u>her</u> having him to dinner' ...

[And letters to Lord Melbourne in which] 'The Queen anxiously hopes Lord M. has slept well … it was very wrong of him not to wish her goodnight … When did he get home? … It was a great pleasure that he came last night &c'.

Bigge explained:

These are examples – I will not trouble you with others. Of course one realises that the Queen was only a girl of 20 [sic. She was in fact eighteen and nineteen] and these letters were written to a man whom she regarded in the light of a father, but still she was Queen and he Prime Minister.

Depend upon it, Her Majesty would never have consented to the publication of these very intimate, may I say, childlike communications – and I repeat again – *cui bono*?

Knollys disagreed and defended their inclusion:

Dear Bigge,
At first I was of the same opinion as you in regard to the publication of Lord Melbourne's letters, but when I found that she was 'carrying on' most of the time with Prince Albert, I thought it would seem that her expressions of affection to the former were simply those of a daughter to one whom she evidently looked upon as a sort of parent. One of her most affectionate letters to Lord M. was written a few days before she told him of her engagement and when she was violently 'in love' with Prince Albert.

I cannot help thinking you are mistaken in supposing that the letters which passed between the Queen and Lord M. will not interest people. I confess to having been much interested in them myself.

In some of this detail, Knollys was mistaken. As can be ascertained from Volume I of the *Letters*, Victoria was only 'carrying on' with Albert after his second visit in October 1839, and they were married four months later. Most of the material to which Bigge objected had been written the year before.

After sending this reply off to Bigge, Knollys conspiratorially wrote to Esher:

> I hold the same opinion [as Bigge] respecting the publication of Lord M.'s letters, but what do you say to the usual way of getting out of a difficulty – a compromise – the compromise being that if Bigge has any particular feelings about any special letters up to 3 or 4 in number, they ought to be omitted.

A compromise was made, removing just one of the entries Bigge objected to and omitting Victoria's letters to Lord Lansdowne. These omissions had little effect on the overall picture of the warm relationship between Victoria and Lord Melbourne.

Bigge was also critical of the decision to typeset the material while it was still being revised. From the proofs he could see that Benson had sent material to the printers containing, for example, the observation that the Duchess of Kent was 'so much pleasanter to deal with now that that man was got rid of' (referring to Sir John Conroy). Although this passage had been marked to be deleted, Bigge thought it highly improper that such sensitive material should ever have been seen by the typesetters. He was a deeply cautious courtier and argued against any 'intimate material' being included:

I always imagined that it was the political correspondence that would be given to the public – for instance all the Prime Ministers' letters, reports of Cabinet meetings, &c tho' of course some of these are included in the papers now under discussion.

I quite see your comparisons of the intervals which separate us from Melbourne and that between James I and Queen Anne, and between Geo II and Queen Victoria. But on the other hand, Queen Victoria has not been dead 6 years – Her memory is loved and venerated by all English-speaking people; in India it is positively a worship – and if I were the King, both from the point of view of son and Mother and also for the sake of the monarchical idea and 'Culte' I would publish nothing which could tend to shake the position of Queen Victoria in the minds of her subjects.

This distinction between personal and public was of course contentious, and was something Benson and Esher had struggled with themselves. In a later letter to Esher, Knollys rather perceptively reminded him that the Queen herself had authorised the publication of many of the Prince Consort's letters in Martin's biography: 'With respect to Bigge's objections, I wonder what the Prince Consort would have said to the publication of his letters and diaries in Martin's *Life*, which remember was brought out under the direct authority of Queen Victoria ...' No doubt he was intending to reassure Esher. Reading Martin today, however, one is struck by how little of the Prince's voice is heard and how few of his personal letters or journal extracts were included. Much of the material comprises letters written about the Prince by others, including Victoria.

Bigge also questioned some of Benson and Esher's editorial decisions, including an apparent attempt to avoid provoking *The Times*. Leopold had often complained to Victoria of the 'scurrilous abuse [heaped] on the Coburg family' by the English press, especially following his marriage to Princess Charlotte, and commended Victoria's principle of not minding what the newspapers said. In a letter written just prior to Victoria's accession, he sought to instruct her about the power of the press and launched an attack – unwarranted, in Benson and Esher's view – on *The Times*. This letter contained a very idiosyncratic but perceptive account of the paper's editorial positions on several political topics, as well of its occasional criticisms of Leopold himself. Benson and Esher must have appended a footnote to this letter criticising Leopold, with which Bigge disagreed. Bigge thought that Leopold's 'severe strictures ... [were] more or less historical' and unobjectionable as they are 'those of a foreign onlooker'. The editors did not agree with him, and only one paragraph of this interesting six-page letter was eventually published, omitting any direct reference to *The Times*.

John Murray may have been behind this decision. The editor of *The Times* had recently begun to publish anonymous articles critical of the production and pricing of the *Letters of Queen Victoria* and accusing Murray of seeking exorbitant profits. Murray launched a libel action against *The Times* and its editor, which was finally concluded in Murray's favour in May 1908.

Meanwhile, Esher privately sounded out his second possible reader, John Morley:

I have finished Vol I and Vol II of *Queen Victoria's Correspondence*, the penultimate revise. It has been difficult work, as, since the book is to be issued by the direct authority of the King, much care must be taken not to allow anything to slip in which can give pain or offence. The latter term in its most catholic sense. Between ourselves, the King wishes you to look through the final proofs. Will you, when asked, consent?

(There is, unsurprisingly, no evidence that Esher actually consulted the King before making this request to Morley.)

On the same day, 17 August 1906, he wrote to John Murray, saying: 'I return the proofs of Volume I. The King has gone through them and by H.M.'s directions I have cut out certain passages.' These deletions were not restricted to Bigge's list and included several long excisions. Murray replied, 'From the editorial point of view the excisions seem to be not serious. From the printer's point of view I fear they will be very serious.' Murray sent a similar letter to Benson, who was at his mother's home at Horsted Keynes, Sussex. In his diary Benson recorded:

20 Aug 1906
Woke feeling better then opened letter from Murray which had arrived on Sat – not new proofs but the King's copy!! Many omissions, some very serious – long serious letter from Murray. Went up to Town to see Murray – went solidly through [it all].

Such lengthy excisions at this stage were a technical nightmare. There were more than a thousand pages already typeset, sitting in trays at the printers. The material to be deleted had to be located in the trays of type and that type removed. A decision had then to be made whether the remaining type should be physically moved up to fill the gaps, or whether alternative text of the same length should be found as a replacement. Either option was time-consuming and expensive, and would have repercussions for the publication dates of the book. It also meant additional work for the indexers, as the indexes for Volume I and II were by now almost complete. After spending half a day with Murray, Benson wrote to Esher:

> I have just been through the proofs with Murray. There are three serious omissions. If these omissions are met simply by closing up the pages, the whole pagination of the book will have to be altered, and the index thrown out of gear. It will mean breaking up every page [of type] from the point of the first alteration [on page 8] to the end of the book – this will waste time and be of course very expensive.
>
> What I would suggest is that we should find some unemphatic passages of letters of a purely historical kind to fill up the gaps – It will be quite easy to do this out of the cancelled proofs or the MSS. The introductions [i.e., the replacement material] need not come chronologically exactly where the omissions come, but a few pages earlier or later; and thus only a few pages need be disarranged ... – but you can trust me to find absolutely colourless passages.

This solution may well have been Murray's. Benson now set about collecting lines of 'absolutely colourless' text. Considering the agony he had felt at having to delete so much interesting material in the earlier stages of the project, he must have felt a huge frustration at this point. But his pragmatism came to the fore; he took Esher at his word and believed that these changes had been requested by the King, and that once they were made they could finally send the book to print.

Meanwhile, Esher had received Morley's response to the proofs:

My dear Esher,

I have read it all with the utmost interest and gratification. Success in biography obviously depends on three things – subject, material and handling.

As for subject, Queen Victoria stands in the first place, for not only was her rank and station illustrious, but her personality was extraordinary – in its vigour, tenacity, integrity, and in the union of all these stubborn qualities with the suppleness and adaptability required from a Sovereign in a Constitutional system.

Second, your material was evidently rich and copious, and I cannot think but that the King was right not to pinch you. I hope the same liberal spirit will help future volumes.

Thirdly, I thoroughly applaud your <u>plan</u>. A biography of the three-decker stamp, filled out with dead history, would have been, I believe a great mistake. I always thought Theodore Martin went too far in that direction. What people want to know, and will always want to know, about Queen Victoria, is her character, her ways in public business, her relations with her Ministers and her times.

You give quite enough in your excellent introduction to the chapters, to let people know where they are; and if they seek more, there are plenty of books already where they can find it.

I have kept a keen look-out, as you wished me to do, for references or quotations that might touch sore places.

I find none such. The air of the whole book is good-natured as it should be and I see nothing to give pain to anybody. It will doubtless be harder to walk quite safely as you come nearer our own day. Meanwhile I feel pretty sure about you. Of course, I do not overlook the responsibility that falls in a special degree upon the King. So far, I do not hesitate to say, if I am any judge, that there is not a line with which from this point of view anybody can quarrel.

The industry and exactitude with which the elucidating notes etc., have been prepared, command my real admiration. I know well how much pain is meant by these things. I have jotted down on a separate piece of paper one or two most minute and trivial points that struck me.

One word I should like to add, though it is not within my commission: don't publish one volume by itself. I am sure, and my publishers agree, that one distinct element in the success of my *Gladstone* was that people sat down to the whole meal at once. You may choose, or may not be able, to do as much as this. But pray try to approach my counsel of perfection, if and in so far as you can.

I congratulate you, dear Esher, on your associations with a book that all the world one day will read, study, admire and greatly like (which is more than admiring) as now does,

Yours most sincerely,

John Morley

Most of Morley's recommendations were corrections to errors in names and titles, and Benson was grateful to have his imprimatur. With Morley's seal of approval, Esher felt he could confidently proceed with Volume I. He promptly sent Morley's letter to the King and suggested that he approve the volume to go to press. The King complied, giving his full consent, albeit briefly:

> Mr Morley's letter is a most cheering and complimentary one. His advice should also be followed and <u>not</u> produce one volume by itself. It is likely to be a great success.
>
> Edward R.I.

Having Morley as a reader was Esher's trump card. King Edward, despite being claustrophobically surrounded by intellectuals and learned men in his boyhood, maintained an admiration for certain men of learning all his life; John Morley was one of them. Finally, on 24 October 1906, after both Benson and Murray had checked it through one last time, the first volume went to be stereotyped. Volume II still awaited the King's approval, and Volume III was yet to be set into type.

Esher now turned his attention to Volmes II and III. He did not seek outside readers for these volumes; he and Knollys would instead act as the King's censors. Although when Esher discussed these final changes with Benson and Murray, he spoke as though they were the King's, correspondence confirms that Esher and Knollys were busy drawing up the 'King's excisions' in Scotland while the King himself was on the Continent.

Benson gently put to Esher that many of the proposed excisions for Volume II were 'quite unnecessary & even pointless & to garble some of the letters very much. I suppose there is no appeal?' Esher forwarded Benson's protest to Knollys, who haughtily replied:

> I return Benson's letters. Literary recluses are not always the best judges of what is good taste in these matters and I

think we have been very indulgent in our excisions. I shall
be curious to know to what particular ones he objects to as
'pointless'. He forgets that the work will be published
under the direct auspices of the King.

Tellingly, Knollys referred to 'our' excisions rather than 'the
King's'. Esher's response to Benson has not been located, but
it was persuasive enough for Benson to acquiesce: 'I quite
see your point about H.M.'s position in the matter.'

Upon his return from holiday, however, Benson had
second thoughts. He tried again to have Esher reconsider the
deletions. He put specific arguments against some of them,
filling nine foolscap pages with a list of the proposed excisions and his objections. For example, some were simply, he
contended, 'historical facts'; others changed the meaning or
intent of the Queen's comments. Esher responded forcefully:

My dear ACB,

I have gone very carefully through your suggested restora-
tions of the original text and have spoken to the King
about them.

H.M. says that it is not a question of 'well known historical facts' or the 'great historical value' of passages. The
point is that this book is published under the King's
authority. Take for instance your suggestion in regard to
page 17. You would not feel that the King would be justified in allowing a passage to be printed in which his
mother characterises a living sovereign, one of the most
respected and a great personal friend of the King, as an
'<u>utter nullity</u>'.

The same class of objection holds good in all cases
where excisions have been made. The principle all along

has been to avoid giving pain to living servants or friends of the King, or umbrage to foreign states. I am sure you will feel that this is the right view, even if the book should suffer, which in my judgment it will not.

Yours always,

E

The 'utter nullity' was the Austrian Emperor. The phrase was not Victoria's; she was repeating to King Leopold an opinion of Tsar Nicholas I, although we can assume it was a view shared by Victoria, Albert and possibly also Leopold. But the reference was not, as Esher suggested, to Emperor Franz Josef, who was indeed a 'great, personal friend' of King Edward VII. It referred to his elderly uncle, Ferdinand I, who became emperor in 1835 and who abdicated during the Revolution of 1848 (to be succeeded by Franz Joseph). He was known to be mentally deficient, so Benson was justified in saying this was 'a perfectly well-known historical fact'. And he had died in 1875, so Esher was wrong to say that the words described a 'living Sovereign'. These misunderstandings confirm that Esher had not in fact 'spoken to the King' about these excisions. For all his shortcomings, Edward VII was pedantic about such personal details and would have corrected Esher on this point (he once sent an equerry to correct Esher's son, Maurice, after Maurice, within the King's earshot, had referred to Nicholas II as 'the Russian Emperor' instead of 'the Emperor of Russia'). Yet again, Esher assumed an authority which in reality he did not have.

But Benson had no further recourse and the sentence was omitted. In making this change, Esher probably had in mind the King's recent visit to Austria, his ongoing friendship with the Austrian royal family and his desire to maintain political peace in Europe. Esher could have simply justified the deletion to Benson on the grounds of European diplomacy, but he chose instead to flaunt his 'superior knowledge' – which in this instance was incorrect.

The excisions ordered from Volume II fall into several categories: those based on political considerations, especially as they might have affected Edward's relationship with his ministers or his European connections; those which showed Victoria to have been excessively assertive, unfeminine or insulting; and those which showed political bias. There was some overlap between these categories; for example, one of the ordered excisions was from Victoria's description of the Irish people during her visit to Dublin in 1849. She described her reception by the Irish crowds to Leopold:

> The most perfect order was maintained in spite of the immense mass of people assembled and a more good-humoured crowd I never saw, but noisy and excitable beyond belief, talking, jumping and shrieking instead of cheering ... you see dirtier, more ragged & wretched people here than I ever saw anywhere else.

The King (or rather, Esher) ordered that the word 'dirtier' be excised, while 'ragged' and 'wretched' were allowed to stay. Benson contested it: 'Why erase?' Later, Victoria also described the Irishwomen as 'handsome', with their 'beautiful black eyes and hair' and 'fine ... teeth'. She was sympathetic to their situation and – in the desperate circumstances of post-famine Ireland – 'dirty' was probably accurate, although perhaps too blunt for the political climate of 1906. Whether the censors excised it because it was offensive to the Irish people or too unfeminine for a Queen is impossible to say.

Benson and Esher had already omitted some of Victoria and Albert's views on Ireland, conscious that it was a sensitive topic. King Edward and Queen Alexandra had made two visits to Ireland as sovereigns, in 1903 and 1904, and the King visited alone in 1907. The great enthusiasm with which they were received raised temporary hopes that, even in an era of ardent Irish nationalism, the monarchy might continue to bind the United Kingdom together. In this climate, some of Victoria's opinions were deemed unpublishable.

In 1848, Victoria had written to Leopold about the Young Irelander movement and their failed uprising that July:

> There are ample means of crushing the rebellion in Ireland, I think it is now very likely to go off without any contest *which people (and I think with right) rather regret. The Irish should receive a good lesson or they will begin again.*

The words in italics were initially included, but were deleted as another of the 'King's excisions'. It seems Esher and Knollys felt that Victoria's call for the Irish to be taught a 'good lesson' was too brutal for public consumption, although, curiously, her opinion that she had 'ample means of crushing the rebellion' was not.

Victoria's views about the French were also softened, probably to avoid offending the King. In 1848, when the French King was forced to abdicate, the royal family – the Orleans – sought refuge in England and were given the use of the Surrey home of their son-in-law, King Leopold. Benson and Esher included some letters from early in 1848, in which Victoria expressed concern for their wellbeing. Elsewhere, however, the Queen was venomously critical of French politics, both monarchical and republican. Edward

VII, in contrast, was known to be very fond of French people and institutions, as was Esher. Several excisions were ordered from Volume II to avoid giving offence. In 1846, contrary to a pledge he had given to Victoria, the French King had pursued what he saw as a diplomatic *coup* involving the marriage of his son to the younger sister of the Queen of Spain. Victoria referred to this 'faithless conduct of the French' in a letter to Leopold, a phrase which was ordered to be excised. Benson argued that stronger language was used in subsequent letters (Victoria went on to rage against the King's 'infamous' and 'very dishonest' behaviour) and that this material was not controversial. The 'Queen's inclination had long been known – the gap will be more suggestive than the excised term,' he pleaded. Nevertheless, it was removed.

In 1848, Louis Philippe was forced to abdicate and escaped, in disguise, to England. Although she did not approve of his decision to flee, Victoria understood it: 'Still the recollection of Louis XVI *and the wickedness and savageness of the French mob is enough to justify all and everybody will admit that.*' The words in italics were deleted, although Benson again protested: 'No cause for excision.' As the political temperature rose, Victoria continued to discuss the situation with Leopold; again, Esher ordered that her harsh criticism of the French people be removed: 'In France, things go on <u>dreadfully</u> *& for the sake of morality there ought to be some great catastrophe at Paris for that is the hothouse of Iniquity from wherein all the mischief comes.*'

Later, upon hearing of the *coup d'état* by Louis Napoleon, Victoria wrote ironically to Leopold: 'I must write a line to ask what you say to the <u>wonderful</u> proceedings at Paris, which is really like a <u>story</u> in a book or a play! What is to be the result of it all?' Victoria's scorn for the 1848 revolutionaries would have been provocative and even dangerous in an era of bloc alliances; Britain had only recently entered the *Entente cordiale* with France, and was hopeful of securing a Triple Entente including Russia (this was eventually achieved in 1907). Although Victoria's remarks referred to earlier French regimes, they might still have been regarded as offensive to the French people, and to her Francophile son.

By 1852, Louis Napoleon had declared himself Emperor for life as Napoleon III. Unmarried, he hoped to find a bride who would secure a useful alliance. One candidate was Princess Adelaide, the sixteen-year-old daughter of Queen Victoria's half-sister, Feodore. Both Feodore and Victoria opposed the marriage, for several reasons. Politically, Victoria, Albert and the government were reluctant to recognise the Second Republic and Napoleon III. Ada would have had to convert to Catholicism. And the Emperor, at forty-four, had already acquired a reputation as a womaniser, which the sisters found distasteful in a prospective husband. Adelaide was in England under Victoria's care at the time. Feodore wrote to Victoria to discuss how to repel the approach by Napoleon III's agent. A month later, Napoleon married Countess Eugenie. Late in the editing process, Benson suggested that these particulars be omitted because of the hurt they might cause Napoleon III's widow, Empress Eugenie, who was still alive and had lived in England. Esher greatly admired Eugenie, and had already approved the letter several times. It remained in the published volume, but with one set of ellipses following Feo's cry: 'If we could just say, "No!" at once! ...' The excision probably included a personal assessment of the Emperor that justified her opinion of his unsuitability.

Victoria's views on Russia were also deemed unfit for publication. King Leopold bore an ongoing distrust of the Emperor of Russia, Nicholas I, which had its origins in the negotiations at the time of the establishment of the constitution for an independent Belgian state. In 1844, the Tsar had just undertaken a very successful visit to Victoria and Albert at Windsor. Benson and Esher included some delightful letters from Victoria, revealing her anxiety about the visit and her subsequent triumph at its success. In early May 1844, she confided in her journal: 'We are still threatened with a visit from the Emperor of Russia which alarms me somewhat ...' On 30 May she continued:

> [Foreign Secretary] Lord Aberdeen came immediately after luncheon and told Albert that <u>after all</u> the Emperor of Russia <u>is</u> coming and may be here on the 3rd! This rather upset me for I so dread the fatigue & hate appearing in my present condition. But it cannot be helped, disagreeable as it is. He will only remain a week.

At the time Victoria was heavily pregnant with her fourth child; despite their usual coyness about such matters, Benson and Esher allowed this veiled reference to pregnancy to remain in the published text.

The Tsar arrived in Windsor at the same time as another distinguished visitor, the elderly King of Saxony. Writing to Leopold, Victoria described the Tsar as a 'striking man' of large physique, with a 'quite fearful' expression 'unlike anything I ever saw before'. He seldom smiled, she said, and when he did 'his expression was *not* a happy one'. Yet, she continued excitedly:

The children are much admired by the <u>Sovereigns</u> – (how <u>grand</u> this sounds!) – and Alice allowed the Emperor to take her in his arms, and kissed him *de son propre accord*. We are always so thankful that they are <u>not shy.</u>

On a political level, she wrote:

If the French are angry at this visit, let their dear King and Princes come; they will be sure of a truly affectionate reception on our part. The one which Emperor Nicholas has received is cordial and civil, mais ne vient pas du coeur [but it doesn't come from the heart].

At the conclusion of the visit, Leopold wrote to Victoria with a warning: 'Concerning great Nick, I must express myself with great care, as I can see that my opinion may be judged as the result of some pique.' He proceeded into a diatribe, accusing the Tsar of not fulfilling his promises and

of displaying great inconsistency in his conduct towards us, for so powerful a Prince ... having consented to the arrangement [of Belgian sovereignty by] four ratifications in his own handwriting, the hostility with which we have been treated is not to be explained.

Secondary states may be forced to swallow unpleasant things from weakness; Constitutional Sovereigns of great countries may be forced by their Parliaments and may make a personal distinction and say officially I must deal with these people, but personally, I will avoid it as much as possible ... But the most powerful Autocrat must either <u>frankly refuse at first</u>, or having consented to the arrangements, must keep up decent form ... The Emperor has

refused <u>all</u> and <u>every</u> acknowledgment of political existence to me and this country. The Polish affair is of so tri-
fling a nature that it excuses nothing.

Without France going with England, Austria cannot
move. But enough of politics. I should not have mentioned
them but I think it wise to be on the most friendly terms
with Russia, without losing sight of what is going on in the
immense sphere of action where the Russians already
move as Masters. If Maria Theresa had been told that
Moldavia Walackia and Servia [sic] would be governed by
the Russians, who at the same time would have nearly the
whole of Poland, she would have been astonished in good
earnest [with good reason].

Benson and Esher omitted nearly all of this letter, but
provided only one set of ellipses (after 'Concerning great
Nick ...'), giving the reader no sense of how much had
been left out. It is a moot question whether, given the political climates of 1844 and 1906, the omissions were for
economy of space or in deference to the King's dictum,
delivered by Esher, that the editors were 'to avoid giving
pain to living servants or friends of the King, or umbrage
to foreign states'.

Leopold was always keen to educate Victoria in history
and royal precedent. The editors included several letters
reflecting this. He was also fond of referring to his first wife,
Charlotte, Princess of Wales, with whom he had lived in
England until her death in childbirth in 1817. In a letter
written to accompany a portrait of Charlotte he was giving
to Victoria, he described Charlotte's life and personality in
detail. Three sentences were ordered for excision; they were
critical not just of Charlotte's father, King George IV, but

also of her grandmother and namesake, Queen Charlotte (the wife of George III), and of the royal family as a whole:

> The power my wishes and arguments had on her [Princess Charlotte] was remarkable; the greatest sacrifice on her part was to be civil to the old Queen and to her father. She knew him but too well; he was very jealous of her, and she feared him without feeling any esteem for him. What you have seen of the remnant of the Royal family may give you a clue of what it was when they were all alive, and still in vigorous dispositions for every descriptions of mischief.

Leopold had never been welcomed into Charlotte's family, so this criticism was not surprising. In another letter – which was published without excisions – he recalled events following the death of Victoria's father and in particular the reprehensible behaviour of George IV (given here with the editors' ellipses and italics):

> [Your Father's] affairs were so deranged that your Mother would have had no means even of leaving Sidmouth if I had not taken all this under my care and management. That dreary journey, undertaken, I think on the 26th January, in bitter cold and damp weather, I shall not easily forget. I looked very sharp after the poor little baby [Victoria], then about eight months old. Arrived in London we were very unkindly treated by George IV, *whose great wish was to get you and your Mamma out of the country* and I must say without *my* assistance you could not have remained … I state these facts because it is useful to remember through what *difficulties* and *hardships* one had to struggle.

Victoria's own criticism of her family was also toned down. One passage ordered for excision concerned her half-brother, Charles, who had been appointed Foreign Affairs Secretary in the new federation of German states. Victoria wrote to Leopold:

> I do not think the fate of the Minor Princes of Germany is so completely decided as Charles, (whose conduct rather reminds me of Egalité in the old French Revolution) is so anxious to make one believe.

She believed Charles to be siding, with indecent enthusiasm, with the revolutionary Frankfort Assembly of 1848, whose more radical members wished to dispossess the minor princes of Germany such as Victoria's brother-in-law, Duke Ernest II of Coburg. She was comparing Charles with Philip Egalité, a relation of Louis XVI who, during the French Revolution, championed (for a time) the cause of the revolutionaries who eventually executed the Bourbon king (Egalité was the father of Louis Philippe, who had just sought refuge in Britain). Why was this comment removed? Charles was Edward VII's uncle; perhaps Esher thought the King would be uncomfortable with such a close relative being described as a revolutionary, even if by Victoria herself.

In seeking to accommodate the idiosyncrasies and potential objections – both known and imagined – of the King, the editors were willing to sacrifice aspects of Victoria's life and personality. These last-minute excisions of material initially approved for publication reveal their anxiety, after waiting so long for royal permission, to have the book published at last.

Conclusion

THE EDITORS' QUEEN

JOHN MURRAY HAD HOPED to publish sometime in 1906, but as time wore on and the courtiers prevaricated, publication was delayed several times. By 2 September 1907 all three volumes were ready to print. The books were finally in the hands of booksellers on 16 October 1907, ready to go on sale, at the price of three guineas, the following day. Murray told Benson happily that five thousand copies had been despatched. Thanks to Murray's strenuous efforts, editions were published simultaneously in America and in translation in France and Germany.

The Letters of Queen Victoria was reviewed widely; Esher collected thirty-seven mostly favourable reviews and had them bound for his archive. Benson recorded a few desultory remarks about the reception in his diary: he was pleased by reviews which praised the editing, but disappointed that among the many letters of congratulations he received, none was from his 'attached friends of Eton'. Discussions began about reprinting almost immediately and a cheaper edition was produced in 1908, priced at one guinea for all three volumes. This 1908 edition, with its smaller format, cloth cover and thirteen plates (compared to the thirty-nine plates of the first edition), is the one most widely found in libraries today.

Not long after publication, Benson had a nervous breakdown and was finally admitted to a clinic in Mayfair in November (after checking the proofs of the preface in September, he had told his diary, 'depression lurks in the background, moving dimly like a figure in a mist'). Esher went on to establish the Royal Archives and to publish extracts of Victoria's girlhood journal in 1912 (Benson, still recovering from his depression, declined to be joint editor and suggested Esher ask Hugh Childers to assist him, which he did).

*

Biographers and historians have drawn on the published letters ever since, treating them as a representative and comprehensive primary source. These letters have shaped our understanding of Victoria's life, and this has led to some serial misrepresentations.

Lytton Strachey's biography of Queen Victoria, which has remained in print since its publication in 1921, is typical. Using Benson and Esher's structure as its template, it describes the young, innocent girl-queen who becomes a wife and mother, with the greatest emphasis placed on the strong men who surrounded her. Six of Strachey's ten chapters focus on these men. His assessment of Victoria's role in the rise and fall of the power of the Crown sums up his depiction of her reign more generally: 'Victoria in effect was a mere accessory.'

The published letters, however, should not be seen simply as 'primary sources'. The personality and outlook of each editor; the need to observe royal protocols and avoid offending living relatives; a desire to avoid controversy and yet to sell books – all of these factors helped to shape the published image of Victoria. As Edwardian gentlemen, the editors approached everything they read through a very particular perspective. This is most evident in the priority they gave to the voices of men. Benson and Esher could 'hear' her male correspondents' voices more clearly and appreciate their importance more readily; Queen Victoria's own words comprise just forty per cent of the published letters, and her many female correspondents appear barely at all. This is not to deny the importance of the men who wrote to Victoria; in omitting her huge correspondence with other women, however, the editors excluded a large part of Victoria's experience.

The image that made most sense to Benson and Esher was that of the elderly teaching the young. They wanted to spin the romantic story of Lord Melbourne and the girl Queen, which, of course, they could readily understand: the senior statesmen, experienced in the world, guiding the youthful Queen with love and wisdom – any flirtatiousness on her part merely confirmed Lord Melbourne's endearing charm upon her. Although the gender is different, it follows that classical Greek model of pedagogy of which they were both enthusiasts.

Acknowledgments

The completion of this book is the result of assistance and support from all of the people who helped with my PhD, the staff at Black Inc., especially Chris Feik and my very perceptive editor, Denise O'Dea, and John Hirst. Not only was he persistent in convincing me that the thesis should be published but he did the initial abridgement to persuade Chris Feik as well. Without his efforts the book would have remained in the thesis.

The professors, lecturers, tutors and postgraduate students of the History Department at La Trobe University in the 1990s and 2000s built a vibrant, intellectual culture providing both research training and stimulus for further endeavour. And it was filled with fun and friendship. I want to thank you all.

I am very grateful to friends for their help, their friendship, hospitality and sustenance, and for sharing the joys of the research: Walter and Charlotte Arnstein, Ingrid Barker, Lady de Bellaigue, Janet Butler, Liz and Richard Coyle, Liz Dimock, Graham Fairhurst, Carole Hamilton-Barwick, Tim Healey, Dr Gustaaf Janssens, Sue Knowles, Robert Lacey, Margaret Lee, Evelyn Maynard, Lee-Ann Monk,

John and Virginia Murray, Keith and Joyce Pescod, Ann and Mike Reece, Sue and Bob Sutton, and Monika Wingrove.

To my first teachers: Mum and Dad, Leah and John Ward; and my brothers and sisters, Graeme, Leah, Ian, Rhonda and Steven, their partners and children.

To our two little grandsons, Mason and Hayden, my new teachers.

To my husband, Roy, and our children, Roy, Leah, Phillip and Allison, who all suffered various degrees of deprivation during my PhD. I hope you will all share in the satisfaction of seeing the book published.

REFERENCES

This book is drawn directly from my PhD dissertation, *Editing Queen Victoria*: *How Men of Letters Constructed the Young Queen*. The thesis is held by the Borchardt Library at La Trobe University in Bundoora, Australia, and is accessible electronically.

The research drew upon material from many libraries and archives:

Aberdeen Papers, British Library Manuscripts Collection, St Pancras, London, England.

Alexandrine, Duchess of Saxe-Coburg, Letters and Papers, Staatsarchiv Coburg, Germany.

Alice, Grand Duchess of Hesse, Letters, Hessische Staatsarchiv Darmstadt, Germany.

Bedford and Tavistock Family Papers, Woburn Abbey, Bedfordshire, England.

Benson Collection, University of British Columbia Library, Vancouver, Canada.

Benson Correspondence and Papers, Department of Manuscripts and University Archives, Cambridge University Library, Cambridge, England.

Benson Correspondence and Papers, Houghton Library, Harvard University, Cambridge, Massachusetts, USA.

Benson Deposit, Department of Western Manuscripts, Bodleian Library, Oxford, England.

Benson Diary, Old Library, Magdalene College, Cambridge, England.

Benson MSS, Special Collection, Charles E. Young Research Library, University of California, Los Angeles, USA.

Borchardt Library, La Trobe University, Bundoora, Victoria, Australia.

Brett Family Autograph Collection, Sydney Jones Library Special Collection, University of Liverpool, England.

British Library Newspaper Collections, Colindale Avenue, London, England.

Buccleuch, Duchess of, Papers and Letters, National Library of Scotland, Edinburgh, Scotland.

Cambridge University Library, Cambridge, England

College of Arms, London, England.

Davidson Papers, Lambeth Palace Library, Lambeth Palace, London, England.

Dona Maria II, Queen of Portugal, Biblioteca Nacional Ministera da Cultura, Campo Grande, Lisbon, Portugal.

Edinburgh Public Library, Edinburgh, Scotland.

Edward VII Coronation Records, Westminster Abbey Muniments Room, London, England.

Elgar Papers, Elgar Birthplace Museum, Lower Broadheath, Worcestershire, England.

Empress Frederick Letters, Kurhessische Haisstiftung, Schloss Fasanerie, Eichenzell, Germany.

Ernest II, Duke of Saxe-Coburg, Staatsarchiv Coburg, Germany.

Esher Papers, Churchill Archives Centre, Churchill College, Cambridge, England.

Eton College Archives, Eton, Berkshire, England.

Feodore, Princess Ernest of Hohenlohe-Langenburg, Letters
Hohenlohe-Zentralarchiv, Neuenstein, Germany.

Fulford Papers, privately held by Lord Shuttleworth, Leck
Hall, Lancashire, England.

Gladstone, Catherine, Diary and Letters, Flintshire Record
Office, Hawarden, Wales.

Gosse Papers, Brotherham Library, Leeds University, Leeds,
England.

Gulbenkian Foundation Library, Lisbon, Portugal.

Lee Papers, English Miscellaneous Collection, Department of
Western Manuscripts, Bodleian Library, Oxford, England.

Lees-Milne Papers, Beinecke Rare Books and Manuscripts
Library, Yale University, New Haven, Connecticut, USA.

Leopold I, King of the Belgians, and Queen Louise of the
Belgians, Archives of the Royal Palace, Brussels, Belgium.

Liverpool Papers, (including letters of Catherine Vernon
Harcourt), British Library Manuscripts Collection, St
Pancras, London, England.

Lyttelton, Lady Sarah, Papers and Letters, privately held by
Lord Cobham, Hagley Hall, Worcestershire, England.

Murray Papers, Letters of Charles Fairfax Murray, John
Rylands Library, Manchester University, Manchester,
England.

Murray Papers and Letters, John Murray Archive, now at
the National Library of Scotland, Edinburgh, Scotland.

Nemours, Duchess of, Letters, Archives Générale du
Royaume, Brussels, Belgium.

Northumberland, Duchess of, Letters and Papers, Bryn-Y-Pys
Collection, Flintshire Record Office, Hawarden, Wales.

Palmerston Papers, Hartley Library Archives and Manuscripts, Southampton University, Southampton, England.

Portuguese Royal Family Papers, Ajuda Palace Archives, the Biblioteca Da Ajuda, Lisbon, Portugal.

Portuguese Royal Family Papers, Casa Real, Institute dos Arquivos Nacionais, Torre do Tombo, Lisbon, Portugal.

Public Record Office, Kew, England.

Queen Victoria Collection, Coronation Regalia, Kensington Palace, London, England.

Queen Victoria Collection, Costume and Decorative Arts Department, Museum of London.

Royal Commission on Historical Manuscripts, London, England.

Stanley, Lady Augusta, Papers and Letters, privately held by Lord Elgin, Broom Hall, Dunfermline, Scotland.

Victoria, Queen, Journals and Letters, Royal Archives, Windsor Castle, Berkshire, England.

*

I wish to acknowledge here the gracious permission of Her Majesty Queen Elizabeth II to research in, and publish extracts from, the Royal Archives at Windsor Castle.

I am also grateful to the many historians, biographers and other writers whose work has informed, enthused and inspired me in both the thesis and this book. References from specific works are listed below.

PREFACE

1   'For over sixty years ...' The beginnings of my research interest in Queen Victoria: Yvonne M. Ward, 'Biographies of Queen Victoria 1901–1991', honours thesis, La Trobe University, 1993, unpublished; and unbeknownst to me at the time, Mike Fassiotto's entertaining PhD,

'Finding Victorias/Reading Biographies, (Victoria, Queen, Reading)', PhD, University of Hawaii, 1992, unpublished.

1   'the published selections of letters ...' Arthur Christopher Benson and Viscount Esher, editors, *The Letters of Queen Victoria. A Selection from Her Majesty's Correspondence between the Years 1837 and 1861*, 3 vols, London, John Murray (1907), 1908.

1   'the Queen as a wife and a mother ...' Yvonne M. Ward, 'The Womanly Garb of Queen Victoria's Early Motherhood: 1840–42', *Women's History Review*, vol. 8, no. 2 (1999), pp. 277–294.

1   'The senior editor was Lord Esher ...' I wish to acknowledge my gratitude to Lord Esher, Lionel Brett; Oliver Everett, Assistant Keeper of the Royal Archives; and the Master and Fellows of Churchill College, Cambridge, for access to the Esher Papers, and for permission to read and quote from them.

1   'his colleague was Arthur Benson ...' I am grateful to the Master and Fellows of Magdalene College for access to the Benson Diary, and for the assistance I have been given by Dr Ronald Hyam and Mrs Aude Fitsimons.

2   'and his prodigious girth ...' Roger Fulford, *Royal Dukes: Queen Victoria's Father and Her 'Wicked Uncles'*, London, Pan Books, 1933, p. 24.

3   'As the Secretary of the Privy Council, Charles Greville ...' Philip Whitwell Wilson, ed., *The Greville Diary Including Passages Hitherto Withheld from Publication*, 2 vols, London, Heinemann, 1927, vol. I, p. 526.

3   'whereby sprigs of holly were pinned to the neckline ...' Elizabeth Longford, *Victoria R.I.*, London (Weidenfeld & Nicolson, 1964), Abacus, 2000, p. 31.

CHAPTER 1

7 'as his biographer James Lees-Milne described …' James Lees-Milne, *The Enigmatic Edwardian: The Life of Reginald, 2nd Viscount Esher,* London, Sidgwick & Jackson, 1986.

7 'It is not in my line …' Lionel Brett, *Our Selves Unknown*, London, Victor Gollancz, 1985, p. 30.

8 'his "private life" had it been known …' William Kuhn, *Democratic Royalism: The Transformation of the British Monarchy 1861–1914*, London, Macmillan, 1996, pp. 61–62.

8 'Esher inevitably became secretary …' Peter Fraser, *Lord Esher: A Political Biography*, London, Hart-Davis MacGibbon, 1973, pp. 68–71, 80–3.

8 'With his understanding of theatre, Esher recognised …' David Cannadine, 'The Context, Performance and Meaning of Ritual: The British Monarchy and the Invention of Tradition, c. 1820–1977', in Eric Hobsbawm and Terence Ranger, eds, *The Invention of Tradition*, Cambridge, Cambridge University Press, 1992, pp. 101–64.

8 'stage for royal events …' Robert Lacey, *Royal: Her Majesty Queen Elizabeth II*, London, Little, Brown, 2002, p. 38.

9 'Esher had another idea …' Quotes throughout are taken variously from Esher MSS Journal, Churchill Archives Centre, Cambridge; Maurice V. Brett, ed., *Journals and Letters of Reginald, Viscount Esher, 1870–1910*, Vols I & II, London, Ivor, Nicolson & Watson, 1934; Oliver, Viscount Esher, ed., *Journals and Letters of Reginald, Viscount Esher, 1910–1930*, Vols III & IV, London, Ivor, Nicolson & Watson, 1938; and Esher Correspondence Files held in the Churchill Archives Centre, Cambridge.

9 'It has been estimated that Victoria wrote an average of two and a half thousand …' Giles St Aubyn, *Queen Victoria: A Portrait*, London, Sinclair-Stevenson, 1991, p. 340.

10   'Victoria had appointed Princess Beatrice ...' For a full account of Beatrice's actions see Philip Magnus, *King Edward the Seventh*, London, John Murray, 1964, pp. 461–2.

13   'Lord Esher had come to know Arthur Christopher Benson ...' Quotations from Benson come from his diary, which is housed in the Old Library, Magdalene College, Cambridge; his letters collected in the Esher Papers and the Murray Archives, formerly at 50 Albermarle Street, London, now in the National Library of Scotland; and from David Newsome, *On the Edge of Paradise, A.C. Benson: The Diarist*, London, John Murray, 1980.

13   'originally written for *Pomp and Circumstance March No. 1* ...' For further details, see Yvonne M. Ward, '"Gosh! Man I've got a tune in my head!" Edward Elgar, A.C. Benson, and the creation of *Land of Hope and Glory*', *The Court Historian*, vol. 7, no. 1, March 2002, pp. 17–41.

19   'with the publisher ... John Murray IV ...' I am grateful to Virginia and John Murray VII for their help and enthusiasm for this research, for alerting me to their finds in the Grantham storage depot, and for making 50 Albermarle Street such a hospitable haven for researchers. For the history of the John Murray publishing house see Humphrey Carpenter, *The Seven Lives of John Murray*, London, John Murray, 2008.

CHAPTER 2

21   'When his son, Reginald Brett, left for Eton ...' Esher had spent much of his first eleven years at home with his French mother (who was '*difficile* and a bit of a trial,' Esher told his son). But he was nevertheless a Francophile *par excellence* and his excellent French, crucial during his diplomatic missions in the First

World War, was attributed to her influence. (Fraser, *Lord Esher: A Political Biography*, pp. 6–8).

22 'arrested development ...' Cyril Connolly, *Enemies of Promise*, Harmondsworth, Penguin, 1979, p. 271–2.

23 'Oscar Wilde's biographer ...' Neil McKenna, *The Secret Life of Oscar Wilde*, London, Century, 2003, p. 248.

23 'Esher's friends congratulated him on his appointment ...' M. Brett, vol. 1, pp. 44, 45.

24 'According to the radical politician ...' quoted in Lees-Milne, p. 45.

24 'Somerset was the second son ...' See H. Montgomery Hyde, *The Cleveland Street Scandal,* London, W.H. Allen, 1976, and more recently in McKenna, pp. 139–46.

24 'I won't believe it ...' Magnus, *King Edward the Seventh*, p. 214.

25 'The Prince's eldest son ...' Theo Aronson, *Prince Eddy and the Homosexual Underworld*, London, John Murray, 1994.

25 'Esher always emerged smelling of roses ...' David Starkey, 'The Modern Monarchy: Rituals of Privacy and their Subversion', in Robert Smith and John S. Moore, eds, *The Monarchy: Fifteen Hundred Years of Tradition*, London, Smith's Peerage, 1998, p. 254.

25 'marriage was ... the best closet ...' Brenda Maddox, *The Marrying Kind: Homosexuality and Marriage*, London, Granada, 1982, p. 14.

26 'the icy shroud of matrimony ...' A phrase used by Brett's friend, George Binning, in reply to a letter of Brett's, quoted in Lees-Milne, p. 47. The phrasing suggests to me that Binning may have been quoting Brett's words back to him.

26 'Christopher Isherwood ...' quoted in Maddox, p. 70.

26 Details of Nellie's diaries from Lees-Milne, pp. 48ff.

28 'It is no accident ...' Maddox, p. 64.

30 'Contemporary research ...' There is a dearth of literature on the psychological makeup of homosexual paedophiles and perpetrators of homosexual incest, but
that which I found would suggest that Regy's relationships with each of his parents and his school experiences contributed to the basis of his subsequent sexual
propensities. See Dennis Howitt, *Paedophiles and Sexual
Offences against Children*, Chichester, England (New York,
J. Wiley), 1995; Mary de Young, *The Sexual Victimization
of Children*, Jefferson, N.C. and London, McFarland and
Coy, 1982, especially 'Paternal Incest,' pp. 73–5 and
'Homosexual Paedophilia,' pp. 141–60; D.G. Langsley,
M.N. Schwartz and R.H. Fairbairn, 'Father–son Incest',
in *Comparative Psychiatry*, vol. 9, 1968, pp. 218–26; J.B.
Raybin, 'Homosexual Incest: Report of a Case involving
Three Generations of a Family', *Journal of Nervous and
Mental Disorders*, vol. 148, 1969, pp. 105–10; Alisdare
Hickson, *The Poisoned Bowl: Sex and the Public School*,
London, Duckworth, 1996.

31 For information on Esher's other children, see Lees-
Milne, p. 70. Oliver acceded to the title upon the death
of his father, but Maurice inherited all of the Scottish
property and was named sole executor. Dorothy Brett, a
painter, made a permanent home in New Mexico with
D.H. Lawrence and his wife, Frieda (see Sean Hignett,
Brett: From Bloomsbury to New Mexico: A Biography, London, Hodder & Stoughton, 1984; Brenda Maddox, *D.H.
Lawrence, the Story of a Marriage*, New York, Simon &
Schuster, 1994). Sylvia married and became 'the
neglected wife of the uncouth and unfaithful' Vyner

Brooke, the last Rajah of Sarawak (Lionel Esher, *Our Selves*, p. 31). She wrote an account of her life, titled *Queen of the Head-Hunters*. Esher had difficult relations with all of his children, their spouses and grandchildren, except for Maurice and his family. See Lees-Milne, pp. 325–9, and Lionel Esher, *Our Selves*, p. 24.

33 'Gladstone also wrote ...' Sir Sidney Lee, *King Edward VII: A Biography*, London, Macmillan, 1925, p. 569.

34 'When Esher died in 1930 ...' Paul Emden predicted that there would be 'many a surprise' in Esher's papers for future generations to discover. Paul Emden, *The Power Behind the Throne*, London, Hodder and Staughton, 1934, p. 294.

CHAPTER 3

37 Biographical details drawn from Newsome, *On the Edge of Paradise*; David Williams, *Genesis and Exodus: A Portrait of the Benson Family*, London, Hamish Hamilton, 1979; and David Newsome, *Godliness and Good Learning: Four Studies on a Victorian Ideal*, London, Cassell, 1961. Newsome was a Headmaster of Wellington College.

39 'constantly reminding themselves what a disappointment they must be ...' Brian Masters, *The Life of E.F. Benson*, London, Chatto & Windus, 1991, p. 27.

40 'They could see no connection between romantic love ...' John Tosh, *A Man's Place: Masculinity and the Middle-Class Home*, New Haven, Conn., and London, Yale University Press, 1999, pp. 190–4.

43 'Ambitious young men grooming "young girls" ...' Betty Askwith, *Two Victorian Families*, London, Chatto & Windus, 1971, p. 121. See also John Tosh, 'Domesticity and Manliness in the Victorian Middle Class: The Family of

Edward White Benson', in Michael Roper and John Tosh, eds, *Manful Assertions. Masculinities in Britain since 1800*, London, Routledge, 1991, pp. 44–73, and Masters, *The Life of E.F. Benson*, pp. 25–8.

51 'Tim Card ... Benson like all members of his gifted family ...' Tim Card, *Eton Renewed: A History of Eton from 1860 to the Present Day*, London, John Murray, 1994, p. 120.

CHAPTER 4

62 'a white chair with pink satin on wheels was used by the Queen ...' The chair is still in the tea-room of the Royal Archives today, where researchers and staff gather each day for a very welcome morning tea.

65 'He was the son of H.C. Childers ...' In the 1840s Childers Senior and his wife, Emily, had gone to the newly established colonial outpost of Melbourne, Australia. He was instrumental in founding the University of Melbourne in 1853 and was its first Vice-Chancellor. Upon his return to England in 1858, he won a seat in the House of Commons, where for twenty-five years he held various Cabinet positions including Home Secretary in 1886. Hugh was born after his parents returned to England. Jean Uhl, *A Woman of Importance: Emily Childers in Melbourne, 1850–1856*, Melbourne, self-published, 1992.

65 'pulling every string for his advancement', Lees-Milne, p. 152.

CHAPTER 5

77 'Although it was written by Theodore Martin ... Victoria contributed substantially ...' Walter Arnstein, *Queen Victoria*, Basingstoke, Palgrave Macmillan, 2003, p. 2.

77 'those two fat volumes ...' Lytton Strachey, *Eminent Vic-*

torians, London, Chatto & Windus, 1918, p. 10.

78 'very much overworked ...' Virginia Woolf, quoted in Ruth Hoberman, *Modernizing Lives: Experiments in English Biography 1918–1939*, Carbondale, Ill., Southern Illinois University Press, 1984, p. 3.

CHAPTER 6

The material for this chapter is drawn from the biographies by Elizabeth Longford and Walter Arnstein; Dormer Creston, *The Youthful Queen Victoria*, London, Macmillan, 1952; and Katherine Hudson, *A Royal Conflict: Sir John Conroy and the Young Victoria*, London, Hodder & Stoughton, 1994.

94 '... psychological warfare in the household ...' Stanley Weintraub, *Victoria: Biography of a Queen*, London, Unwin Hyman, 1987, p. 86.

95 'In 1836, Feodore hid a note to the Duchess of Northumberland ...' An exciting find in the Northumberland Papers in the Flintshire Record Office, Hawarden, Wales.

CHAPTER 7

103 'wicked Hanoverian uncles ...' Fulford, *Royal Dukes*.

104 'The youngest child of his generation ...' of the Coburg family: See Theo Aronson, *The Coburgs of Belgium*, London, Cassell, 1968; Dulcie Ashdown, *Victoria and the Coburgs*, London, Robert Hale, 1981; for his mother: Augusta, Duchess of Saxe-Coburg-Saalfeld, *In Napoleonic Days, Extracts from the private diary of Augusta, Duchess of Saxe-Coburg-Saalfeld, Queen Victoria's Maternal Grandmother, 1806–1821*, selected and translated by HRH Princess Beatrice, London, John Murray, 1941.

105 'the Portuguese queen, Dona Maria da Gloria II in

1836 ...' For more on the Portuguese Monarchy see V. De Bragança Cunha, *Eight Centuries of Portuguese Monarchy: A Political Study*, London, Stephen Swift, 1911; A.H. de Olivier Marques, *History of Portugal Vol. II: From Empire to Corporate State*, New York, Columbia University Press, 1972, pp. 1–70; Francis Gribble, *The Royal House of Portugal*, London, Eveleigh Nash, 1915.

CHAPTER 8

111 'Born in 1819, Albert ...' Hector Bolitho, *Albert, Prince Consort*, London, David, Bruce and Watson (1964), revised 1970, p. 19.

111 'The possibility that Albert was not ...' David Duff, *Victoria and Albert*, London (Frederick Muller, 1972), Victorian and Modern History Club edition, 1973, pp. 28–32, 66.

112 'Theodore Martin ... quoted Duchess Louise ...' Theodore Martin, *The Life of the Prince Consort*, vol. 1, London, Smith, Elder & Co., 1875, 1880, p. 3.

112 'This marriage "soon broke" ...' Bolitho, *Albert, Prince Consort*, p. 20.

113 'The "natural" state of conjugal life ...' Dona Maria da Gloria II of Portugal to Queen Victoria, quoted in Yvonne M. Ward, 'Queen Victoria and Queen Dona Maria II da Gloria of Portugal: Marriage, Motherhood and Sovereignty in the Lives of Young Queens Regnant (1828–1853)', *Lilith: A Feminist History Journal*, vol. 11 (November 2002), pp. 117–30.

113 'Ferdinand's title of King ...' I am grateful to Dr Sally Godwin-Austen for alerting me to this provision. Details in my article above.

113 'Although Victoria was Queen ... the word "obey" ...' Martin, *The Prince Consort*, vol. 1, p. 72.

113 'Lord Palmerston recognised the dilemma ...' quoted in Cecil Woodham-Smith, *Queen Victoria: Her Life and Times (1819–1861)*, vol. 1, London, Hamish Hamilton, 1972, p. 252.

113 'Victoria attempted to establish Albert unequivocally as head of household ...' C. Grey, *The Early Years of His Royal Highness the Prince Consort*, London, Smith, Elder & Co., 1869, pp. 293–4.

114 'the defining elements of nineteenth-century masculinity ...' John Tosh, 'What Should Historians Do with Masculinity? Reflections on Nineteenth-Century Britain,' *History Workshop*, vol. 38 (1994), p. 184.

115 'stupid Prince George ...' from Queen Victoria's Journal, cited by Longford, *Victoria R.I.*, p. 146. Queen Anne's consort, George of Denmark, was the most recent precedent but the situations were hardly comparable as the roles of monarchs varied even more than those of their consorts throughout and after the Early Modern period. Also Prince George had his own royal title as Prince of Denmark; Albert did not have a royal title.

115 'Lord Melbourne wryly observed ... that the consort of a queen was "an anomalous animal" ...' quoted in *Queen Victoria's Journal*, 27 January, 1840.

115 'requires that the husband ...' quoted in Martin, p. 74.

116 'Albert aimed to exercise "personal power unparalleled by any Consort" ...' Robert Rhodes James, *Albert, Prince Consort: A Biography*, London, Hamish Hamilton, 1983, p. 111.

117 'Ernest reported ... a quiet, happy but inglorious ...' Unpublished letter, Prince Ernest to King Leopold, Dated 1 May 1840, Coburg Archives, 567/WE22:66.

118 'When a woman is in love, her desire for power becomes less and less ...' Hector Bolitho, *Albert the Good*, London, Cobden-Sanderson, 1932, p. 86.

118 'For Albert there was no doubt that a Queen reigning …' Monica Charlot, *Victoria: The Young Queen*, Oxford, Blackwells, 1991, p. 191. See also Chapters 11 and 12.

118 'In June, an assassination attempt …' Reports of the attempt were included by Benson and Esher, *Letters of Queen Victoria*, vol. I: Palmerston to Victoria, 10 June 1840; letters from the King of the French, and Lord Melbourne, 11 June 1840; from King Leopold, 13 June 1840. For more on the assassination attempts see Grey, *The Early Years*, pp. 316–8, which gives Albert's version of the first attempt. See also F.B. Smith, 'Lights and Shadows in the Life of John Freeman', *Victorian Studies*, vol. 30, no. 4 (1987), pp. 459–73; and Trevor Turner, 'Erotomania and Queen Victoria: Or Love among the Assassins?' *Psychiatric Bulletin*, vol. 14 (1990), pp. 224–7, which lists each of the seven assassination attempts and analyses them. On Victoria's escape: RA VIC/Y 32/39 & 32/41. Maria to Victoria, 5 July 1840. On Maria's escape: Torre do Tombo, Caixa 7324 CR/200–10. 'It makes me shudder to think how narrowly you have escaped such great danger on the day of the riot' – Victoria to Maria, 16 May 1847.

118 'Following this attack, and with all parties being aware of the perils of childbirth …' In the 1840s, the mortality rate was conservatively estimated to be five maternal deaths per thousand live births. Pat Jalland, *Death in the Victorian Family*, Oxford, Oxford University Press, 1996, p. 46. Victoria was familiar with several tragic cases. In 1816, Leopold, as Prince of Saxe-Coburg-Gotha, had married Charlotte, the Princess of Wales, the only legitimate grandchild of King George III and Queen Charlotte. After suffering several miscarriages she died at the age of twenty-two, following the difficult delivery of

a stillborn son. There was a huge outpouring of public grief upon her death, monuments were erected in her memory, and one of her physicians committed suicide three months later. Linda Colley, *Britons: Forging the Nation 1707–1837*, London, BCA, 1992, pp. 220–1, 270–2 and Longford, *Victoria R.I.*, pp. 150–1.

Baron Stockmar had been present at Charlotte's death, and although this had occurred two years before Victoria's own birth, she knew about Charlotte's demise and the dangers of childbirth. In her journal, she recorded a discussion with Lord Melbourne in 1838 concerning Princess Charlotte, her life, her happiness with Leopold, and her tragic death. See Longford, *Victoria R. I.*, p. 150, and Esher, *Girlhood Journal*, p. 278. It is now believed that Charlotte may have suffered a form of the disease porphyria, inherited from her grandfather, George III, which would have made her very susceptible to complications in childbirth. Ida McAlpine and Richard Hunter, *George III and the Mad-Business*, London, Pimlico (1969), 1995, pp. 241–6.

In 1839 Princess Marie of Württemberg, merely six years older than Victoria, had died of tuberculosis several months after the birth of a son. She was a sister of King Leopold's second wife, Louise, and had married Prince Alexander, one of Leopold's nephews. There is no direct mention of the cause of her death in Benson and Esher, but Leopold wrote to Victoria that Alexander's position 'puts me in mind of my own in 1817'. Benson and Esher, *Letters of Queen Victoria*, vol. I, 11 and 18 January 1839.

118 'I am to be Regent …' Hector Bolitho ed., *The Prince Consort and His Brother: Two Hundred New Letters*, London, Cobden-Sanderson, 1933, p. 21, Albert to Ernest, 17 July 1840.

119 'Melbourne was delegated to raise the matter with Victoria …' Quoted in Longford, *Victoria R.I.*, p. 163. The Bill was passed on 13 July 1840.

119 'The spirit of the age …' Charlot, p. 189.

119 'I wish you could see us …' Bolitho, p. 31.

120 'By May Victoria was again pregnant …' For details see Roger Fulford, editor, *Dearest Child: Letters between Queen Victoria and the Princess Royal, 1858–61*, London, Evans Bros, 1964, p. 147, Victoria to her daughter Vicky, 27 November 1858; and Ward, 'The Womanly Garb of Queen Victoria's Early Motherhood', pp. 285–6.

120 'Following a debate in the House of Commons, Melbourne …' Arnstein, pp. 44–5.

121 'to prepare the ground …' Longford, pp 168–70.

122 'which suggests that Victoria was not happy …' Charlot, pp. 199–204.

122 'Albert was made chairman …' Martin, *Prince Consort*, vol. I, pp. 118–9.

122 'caricatures of English aristocrats …' Charlot, pp. 203–4.

123 'The response had been very different when Queen Adelaide …' *Dictionary of National Biography* entry for Queen Adelaide (1855), reprinted in Frank Prochaska, *Royal Lives: Portraits of Past Royals by Those in the Know*, Oxford, Oxford University Press, 2002, pp. 116–8.

123 '(falsely) accused of political meddling …' Arnstein, pp. 96–7.

CHAPTER 9

125 'Benson described a set of letters from Princess Feodore …' Some of her letters were published in Harold Albert, *Queen Victoria's Sister: The Life and Letters of Princess Feodore*, London, Hale, 1967.

127 'House of Saxe-Coburg as the stud farm of Europe ...'
    Aronson, *The Coburgs of Belgium,* p. xvi.

129 'Particular aspects of pregnancy and childbirth ...' See
    Judith Schneid Lewis, *In the Family Way: Childbearing in
    the British Aristocracy 1760–1860,* New Brunswick, Rut-
    gers University Press, 1986; and Pat Jalland, *Women,
    Marriage and Politics, 1860–1914,* Oxford, Oxford Uni-
    versity Press, 1988.

129 'arriving in Edinburgh in the first week of September
    ...' see details in Alex Tyrrell, with Yvonne M. Ward,
    '"God Bless Her Little Majesty": The Popularising of
    Monarchy in the 1840s', *National Identities,* vol. 2, no. 2
    (2000), pp. 109–25.

130 'In their discussions of motherhood the two women hid
    ...' For an exploration of the hiding of emotions and anx-
    ieties in motherhood, see Susan Maushart, *The Mask of
    Motherhood: How Mothering Changes Everything and Why
    We Pretend It Doesn't,* Sydney, Vintage Books, 1997.

131 'I think much more of our being like a cow ...' Fulford,
    Dearest Child, p. 115. Other examples p. 94 and pp. 77–8.
    See also Elizabeth K. Helsinger, 'Queen Victoria and
    the "Shadow Side" of Marriage,' in Elizabeth K. Hels-
    inger, Robin Lauterbach Sheets and William Veeder,
    eds, *The Woman Question: Defining Voices, 1837–1883,* vol.
    I, New York, Garland, 1983, pp. 63–77.

132 'Maria and Victoria both adhered absolutely to the idea
    of patriarchy ...' But as Marina Warner pointed out, for
    Victoria, 'however hard she schooled herself in adora-
    tion and abnegation, her natural spirit did not bend
    altogether, and some of the family pleasure – and pain
    – originated with her'. Marina Warner, *Queen Victoria's
    Sketchbook,* London, Macmillan, 1979, p. 137.

CHAPTER 10

135 'Before long it became clear ...' George Plumpetre, *Edward VII*, London, Pavilion books, 1995. Brodrick's account given in his memoirs is quoted p. 143. See also Plumpetre's critique of Esher and his behind-the-scenes activities, pp. 134ff, especially 139. Arthur Benson also heard Brodrick make these complaints: Benson Diary, Old Library, Magdalene College, Cambridge, vol. 49, 16 March 1904.

136 'Queen Victoria's letters revealed to Esher ...' As Reginald Brett, Esher had published *Yoke of Empire: Sketches of the Queen's Prime Ministers*, London, Macmillan, 1896, which he dedicated not to the Queen but to 'The Queen's Youngest Prime Minister', Rosebery.

136 'Certainly the work done by her and the P. Consort ...' M. Brett, *Journals and Letters*, vol. II, p. 97.

137 'This was history with a purpose: to show present-day ministers ...' At a time when the House of Commons was becoming very powerful, Esher sought to bolster the position of the monarch. See William M. Kuhn, *Democratic Royalism*, pp. 72–8.

137 'Palmerston had become a major figure in international ...' Much of the following detail is drawn from Brian Connell, *Regina vs Palmerston: The Private Correspondence between Queen Victoria and Her Foreign Minister, 1837–1865*, New York, Doubleday, 1961, and Arnstein, *Queen Victoria*, pp. 87–96.

138 'He secured the independence of the Belgian throne ...' See the correspondence between King Leopold and Palmerston from 1831–65 in the Archives of the Royal Palace, Brussels and Palmerston Papers, Hartley Library Archives and Manuscripts, Southampton University.

142 'Palmerston never forgave him ...' Longford, *Victoria R.I.*, p. 223. Longford gives a lively account of 'The Devil's Son' through Victoria and Albert's eyes, pp. 214ff.

143 'Pilgerstein ...' Longford, p. 224.

CHAPTER 11

145 'If Esher were to incur the King's disapproval ...' See Lees-Milne, pp. 79–81, 150–2, and 154ff, for descriptions and analyses of the relationships between Esher, Knollys and the King.

148 'The first was Arthur Bigge ...' Paul Emden, *The Power Behind the Throne*, pp. 199–210. In the Birthday Honours of 1910 he was awarded a KCB and the title Lord Stamfordham by King George V. In 1906 he signed his letters 'Bigge' and was referred to as such by Knollys and Esher.

148 'The second was John Morley ...' Magnus Magnusson, ed., *Chambers Biographical Dictionary*, Chambers, Edinburgh, 1990, p. 1042. See also D.A. Hamer, *John Morley: Liberal Intellectual in Politics*, Oxford, Clarendon Press, 1968. Esher had asked Morley, as a friend, to take on his eldest son, Oliver, as an assistant secretary in December 1905, and Morley had obliged. Lees-Milne, pp. 153–4.

163 'In 1848 Louis Philippe was forced to abdicate ...' For details of the experiences of his wives, daughters and grandchildren and Victoria's assistance to them see Yvonne M. Ward, '1848: Queen Victoria and the *Cabinet d'horreurs*', in Kay Boardman and Christine Kinealy, eds, *1848: The Year the World Turned?*, Newcastle, Cambridge Scholars Press, 2007, pp. 173–188.

164 'Victoria's scorn for the 1848 revolutionaries ...' For
political context see Simon Heffer, *Power and Place: The
Political Consequences of King Edward VII*, London, Weidenfeld & Nicolson, 1998, p. 132ff.
172 'Victoria in effect was a mere accessory ...' Lytton Strachey, *Queen Victoria*, London, Chatto & Windus (1921)
1937, p. 125.

INDEX